T0276292

THE
AMERICAN
FOOTBALL
REVOLUTION

BEN ISAACS

THE AMERICAN FOOTBALL REVOLUTION

How Britain Fell in Love with the NFL

First published by Pitch Publishing, 2023

Pitch Publishing
9 Donnington Park,
85 Birdham Road,
Chichester,
West Sussex,
PO20 7AJ
www.pitchpublishing.co.uk
info@pitchpublishing.co.uk

© 2023, Ben Isaacs

A CIP catalogue record is available for this book
from the British Library.

ISBN 978 1 80150 465 2

Typesetting and origination by Pitch Publishing
Printed and bound in India by Thomson Press

Contents

To my parents and siblings for constantly buying me NFL presents when I was a child.

To Amanda for being the most supportive, understanding and amazing wife I can imagine.

To Eliot for being the best daughter in the world and part of the new generation of NFL fans. One day all this will be yours.

Introduction

THE NFL in 1982. There were 28 teams. There was a franchise in Baltimore, but it was the Colts not the Ravens. There was a franchise in Houston but it was the Oilers (later renamed the Titans) not the Texans. The franchise in Washington was known as the Redskins not the Commanders. There were no teams representing Jacksonville, Carolina, Las Vegas, Arizona or Tennessee but there were teams in St Louis (Cardinals) and San Diego (Chargers).

Almost every stadium in use in 1982 has been demolished since then. A small number of teams such as the Bills, Chiefs and Saints have stayed in the same stadium the entire time. The Bears and Packers have practically rebuilt their stadiums from the ground up while staying put – although in 1982 the Packers were playing multiple home games in Milwaukee and looking at the possibility of permanently relocating away from Green Bay.

The biggest story of the year was a massive players' strike that wiped out nearly half the season and forced the league to temporarily restructure the standings and playoffs. There was a mood of doom and gloom in the media and it was suggested that the NFL's popularity had been so dented by the strike that ratings and attendances would plummet over the next decade.

It's fair to say a lot has changed since then.

But the biggest thing that happened for the NFL in 1982 was happening in the UK. The arrival of a weekly NFL highlights show on a brand new TV channel ushered in an era of international growth for the league that is still happening today. Although the NFL has gone from strength to strength within its home market, the people running the league were savvy enough to know there were countries around the globe that could potentially provide extra revenue streams. It's a big world, after all.

The UK – not Canada or Mexico – has become the NFL's second home. Much of that is because of the work done by the NFL and its broadcast partners to put the game in British homes and stadiums. But this only goes so far without the fans.

Plenty of sports have attempted to get a foothold in the UK but remained an afterthought. Not the NFL. The UK's NFL fans fell in love with the sport in the 1980s and a small hardcore kept it alive when most decided it was just a passing fad. They supported a weekly newspaper and started up fan clubs when they felt the mainstream media had lost interest. They would not let the sport die.

They threw their weight behind local teams in the World League of American Football [WLAF] and NFL Europe even when the odds seemed stacked against them. They didn't just play the *John Madden Football* video games, they studied them to learn more about the sport and the players. They figured out how to play fantasy football then enlisted their friends, getting together on Sunday nights to share the love of the game.

They started NFL podcasts tailored to British fans and welcomed everyone. They used social media to make lifelong connections when no one in their neighbourhood was hooked on the sport like they were. They took epic road trips and told everyone who would listen how incredible the atmosphere inside and outside the stadium is at an NFL game, while demonstrating their knowledge and passion to Americans. They brought fans from all across the UK and beyond together for each NFL game in London.

When NFL fans in the UK felt abandoned by the league decades ago, they rolled up their sleeves and created a support network of their own. It's the fans who deserve the most credit for the sport's massive popularity in the UK. These are their stories.

If you're a British fan of the NFL you will see yourself in at least one person in this book. You'll read about people who remind you of friends and family who either got you into the sport or you helped start watching the game.

If you're an American you'll discover how the most 'American' of all your sports became an unlikely cultural export and see how the things you've taken for granted had to be earned by those based overseas. How the very Americanness of the game has been a selling point even at times when the country has been painted in a negative light internationally.

God bless American football.

Foreword

By Mike Carlson

WATCHING THE growth of popularity of American football in the UK has been something remarkable for me, and something in which I've been very glad to have played a small part. When I came to London in 1977, there was little football on the screen. The BBC might show highlights of the Rose Bowl, billed, incorrectly, as the 'university championship' and I seem to recall Super Bowl highlights, in surreal edits, on ITV. I wasn't distraught; I'd begun following cricket and rugby (my ability to write a cricket story got me made sports editor of the news agency for which I worked: 'it's a game; games are easy to understand', was how I explained it to the Welsh editor. I edited hundreds of football (the sport the English who called rugby 'rugger' called 'soccer') matches so I got familiar with that. Later, when I spent eight years with ABC Sports, I covered just about every sport imaginable.

By then, of course, the NFL had begun on Channel 4. I knew Adrian Metcalfe, the head of sport on the channel, whose remit was to provide 'minority' sport, and he considered it somewhat of a coup that he'd hijacked that remit into an entertainment blockbuster. The real key to the burst of popularity of that early show was scheduling: the week-old edited game package ran on Sunday afternoon, after the pubs had closed and the Sunday roasts had been consumed. It was up against shows like *Songs of Praise* and *Antiques Roadshow*, and it was an explosion of colour and excitement. This was at a time when soccer was in its doldrums, nothing like a beautiful game at all, all tugging and fouling and riots in the stands. The effect was immediate, and after a few seasons, powerful enough to bring the Super Bowl champion, Chicago Bears to Wembley, with William 'Refrigerator' Perry to catch the media's attention, to play an exhibition before a sold-out crowd.

The impact of the NFL wasn't just on the fans. Look at what the English Premier League did when they started. If, in 1980, I had told you that soccer matches would be played in all-seater stadia, players would wear squad numbers with their names on the backs of jerseys, that games would start at times other than 3pm on Saturday (especially *Monday Night Football*) and that shows like *The Boot Room* would begin analysing soccer as if it were a game of strategy and tactics, not just 'a bunch of lads who had bottle and weren't unlucky', you would have called me crazy. But they paid attention to what was going on with their audience.

I began doing commentary on Screensport, while I was working for Major League Baseball, involved in the same promotional business in Europe as the NFL, NBA and NHL. I had done baseball analysis with Nick Halling as the host. Nick, who had edited an American football magazine, and I did WLAF games together in that league's second season including live broadcasts from Wembley. Nick said all you needed to do a good call was 'information and water', and I discovered from the live producer, NBC's Ted Nathanson, that you also needed to pay attention to what you saw live that the audience didn't see on screen.

When the Monarchs returned on Sky in 1995, Nick and I covered games live, two a weekend, and I worked on *End Zone* with Kevin Cadle and Gia Milinovich. I began hosting the NFL on Sky, with Nick as my analyst, which made sense only to Sky. Here I discovered one more talent: being able to talk coherently while someone was screaming in your ear! I also did some baseball for Sky, and at one point was barracked by a producer for changing her scripts. An executive was dispatched to scold me, and I explained I hadn't changed the scripts, merely corrected errors as I read them off the autocue. After a moment's silence as he put that together, he then said: 'It doesn't matter if it's wrong; it's only American sports, no one will notice.' 'Except whoever does,' I replied, marking my Sky card for not the final time.

In 1997, Kev took over hosting on Sky, and I was lucky enough to be able to assume the analyst role on Channel 5's late-night live games, though I continued doing NFL Europe for Sky for a few years. This turned out to be a blessing, on both counts. NFL Europe was a perfect proving ground: coaches like Jack Bicknell, Jim Criner and Ray Willsey were open about their teams, and the access to assistants and players, down to watching practice on the fields, was always a learning experience. And late-night NFL was, for me, the perfect format to perform. Filling the commercial breaks with analysis, and the good old-fashioned telestrator, with its chalk-line pencil, let me explain things that the broadcast comms didn't (this was harder with the best analysts, like John Madden or Cris Collinsworth). The late hours and relaxed presentation meant I was free to 'perform' a little – taking in emailed 'Ask Mike' questions about non-football topics – and come up with things like odd nicknames that would liven up the broadcast.

From the start, my perception was that the UK audience was made up of people who were at least attracted to the sport, but who were also sports fans in general, intelligent enough to follow 'games' and therefore able to understand the finer points if they could be explained without jargon, without trying to sound like you were an NFL coach. When a Fox exec praised my colour comms on WLAF, I had asked him for a job in the US; he told me I was not an ex-player, I countered by saying my playing résumé was exactly the same as Bill Belichick's: varsity football and lacrosse at Wesleyan. I even offered to change my name to Mike Cosell.

For Channel 5, on Mondays I would spend two hours spooling through edits of the Sunday games on VHS tapes, hand-scribbling scripts timed to the highlights, which led to things like doing a Ravens' game's highlights as Edgar Allan Poe's poem (*You may question. You may carp. Get hot quotes from Shannon Sharpe. But a touchdown's worth of offense is no closer than before. And if you wish to know the day, When you'll hear on the P.A., that magic incantation 'Touchdown Baltimore', Quoth the Ravens 'Nevermore'.*)

We did a segment called 'Inside The Huddle' to preview the games, which Sky later borrowed. It was five minutes long and had to be done in one take because the 'bubble' music under the voice-over couldn't be edited. I got an email from a sports executive saying I read autocue better than anyone he'd ever seen; my eyes never moved. 'That's cuz we can't afford autocue,' I told him. 'It's all ad lib!' Our audience was enthusiastic, or else they wouldn't be staying up late (or taping it; Colin Murray's phrase when we worked together was 'sleeping baggers vs tapers'), there were a lot of students, a lot of shift workers who wanted something lively, and a lot of people who wanted to feel like they were part of the show. I think the greatest praise I ever received was when someone described me as 'the favourite uncle your parents always seem a little wary of'. I was lucky to work with great hosts: Mark Webster, Nat Coombs, Colin, Danny Kelly and Gary Imlach, all of whom indulged me and were great at making two-way banter.

The big change came when new commissioner Roger Goodell ended NFL Europe and replaced it with the International Series of games from the regular season. The UK audience had soured on exhibitions and outgrown the league, which was great for player development but less good for promoting the NFL itself. British sport could take a page from Goodell's book; the International Series has been a major factor in spreading NFL to a wider audience; three or four sell-outs a year in London means there is a very large committed audience out there. Until recently I would do those live games, and the Super Bowl, on the BBC with Chappers [Mark Chapman] or Nat, Osi [Umenyiora] and J-Bell [Jason Bell], and although I loved working with them and the shows, I thought, were great, my favourite moment was often when I'd meet some fans outside the stadium who would greet me like a friend, and thank me for getting them into the game way back when. It makes it all worthwhile, and I thank them for their support, and thank Ben for putting the spotlight on them.

* * *

Read more from Mike at patreon.com/mikecarlsonfmte and follow him on Twitter @Carlsonsports

The NFL lands on UK TV screens

THE 1982 NFL season is best known in America for a devastating player strike that meant the regular season had to be shortened from a planned 16 games to just nine. In the UK, however, it is Year Zero. It marked the debut of Channel 4's weekly NFL highlights show, simply titled *American Football*, and for many sports fans such as Nick Roworth, life would never be the same again.

Channel 4 launched on 2 November 1982 as the UK's second commercial network. The plan was for it to be distinctive, innovative, experimental and creative. There was a desire to give the British viewers something different, and five days later the channel did just that when it began broadcasting NFL highlights. There was just one problem. The league was now on strike and no games had been played since 20 September. It didn't matter. With the league being pretty much unknown in the UK, Channel 4 was able to show highlights from earlier in the season without it causing a problem. The NFL resumed on 20 November and by the end of the month, Channel 4 was up to date. If you can use the phrase 'up to date' when the highlights they showed on a Sunday afternoon were all a week old.

Channel 4 wasn't devoting much time to the NFL but to be fair it didn't broadcast for many hours at this point. On weekdays Channel 4 would come on air at 4.45pm; it was an earlier start on the weekends but it would still be after lunchtime. However, the channel still found space in its schedule to devote 90 minutes of highlights to the New Year's Day 1983 Rose Bowl game between UCLA and Michigan just 24 hours after it had been played. Bizarrely, at that point in time, a college football game had been afforded more time than any single NFL game in British broadcasting history.

The sport was unlike anything else shown in the UK in the early 1980s. For Nick, this was part of the appeal of following the game: to be different and stand out from the pack. He wasn't surrounded by others who loved the game. His family were dedicated Manchester United fans who thought American football was stupid. This only encouraged him to lean into his rebellious streak and fired his love for the game. 'There were always people comparing it to rugby and moaning about the players wearing pads,' says Nick. 'I would tell them the pads meant they could be more athletic without hurting themselves.'

The first Super Bowl – and thus the first live NFL game – to be shown in the UK was on 30 January 1983, broadcast from 10.45pm to 2.30am. Nick, like many other pioneers, stayed up for all of it. 'I was watching all through that first season,' says Nick, 'and watched the entirety of Super Bowl XVII. My main memory of that game is John Riggins just running for what seemed like forever on that one play.' The 43-yard touchdown run in the fourth quarter by the game's MVP was the most iconic moment of the season. It gave the Washington Redskins their first lead of the game against the Miami Dolphins, and they would eventually hold on to win 27-17. The night created a lot of Washington fans across the UK. Nick was not one of them. He had decided to be a Green Bay Packers fan. 'I don't know why I started supporting the Packers,' says Nick, 'but possibly because they wore green. It's certainly not because I like cheese. I don't even eat cheese. The teams that people usually supported back then were the ones who were big at that time. Those were the ones shown most often on TV and you could buy their T-shirts. The Packers were not one of those!'

It wasn't an easy time to be a Packers fan. The team hadn't won a postseason game since Vince Lombardi left in the aftermath of Super Bowl II. They snuck into the temporarily expanded 1982 playoffs in the first year of Channel 4 highlights despite amassing just five wins but were eliminated in the first round. At this point, Bart Starr, MVP of the first two Super Bowls, was still the starting quarterback; a rare link between those crucial games in the sport's history and its breakthrough in the British sporting landscape. Green Bay wouldn't win a playoff game until a Wild Card victory in January 1994 but Nick had stayed loyal through those many barren seasons. This was despite the NFL not making the Packers one of the teams they promoted through merchandise in the UK during the 1980s. 'I had to send off for Packers stuff,' says Nick. 'By the 90s I finally got a Packers hat. My friend, who's also a Green Bay fan, really likes that hat just because it looks so old now.' His goal was to eventually see his beloved team in the flesh. It would be a long wait.

As a Green Bay fan in 1982, Nick quickly picked up on the team's rivalries. He certainly had no love for the Minnesota Vikings but he inadvertently ended up very close to that team. History was made on 6 August 1983 when the Vikings faced the St Louis Cardinals in front of about 33,000 spectators at London's Wembley Stadium. It wasn't organised or promoted by the NFL itself, but instead by British businessman John Marshall with the blessing of the league's forward-thinking commissioner Pete Rozelle. Marshall was ahead of his time and felt that the NFL could go worldwide with games in Tokyo, Milan, Paris and Munich after its London debut.

(Milan and Paris haven't had the NFL experience but Tokyo has hosted plenty of preseason games, including one back in 1976, while Munich celebrated its first regular season game in 2022.) The title sponsor was the short-lived, Missouri-based Global International Airways and the game itself was billed as the Global Cup.

'A few of my colleagues were interested in the NFL,' says Nick. 'I can't remember how we found out about the game at Wembley but we managed to get tickets. One of my colleagues had lived in San Diego, so he supported the Chargers. This was my first visit to Wembley and I couldn't believe the awful state that the stadium was in. We were sitting on terrible wooden benches. I was shocked that this was our national stadium. It really was dismal. We ended up sitting right behind the Vikings' bench. It's the only time in my life I've ever pulled for the Vikings.'

Nowadays NFL games at the new Wembley Stadium, Twickenham Stadium or Tottenham Hotspur Stadium sell out very quickly. This was not the case for the Global Cup. 'It just seemed empty,' says Nick. 'Because of the Vikings players on the sideline, our view was terrible. We told the stewards about it and at the end of the first quarter they let us switch seats. We were allowed to sit in a much better section because there was no one there. This area had proper flip-down seats so we were finally comfortable and could see the game.'

The *New York Times* reported on the game, describing the Vikings' 28-10 win as a 'hit'. They interviewed some fans outside, however, who were not thrilled by what they had seen. According to their report, Dai Cartwright from Cardiff described the stop-start nature of the game as 'a bit disappointing', adding that, 'People here complain about having advertisements at half-time in soccer because it breaks up the atmosphere.' The report also included a quote from an American who attended. Bruce Kelm told the newspaper's reporter: 'I thought I'd get my revenge for the way my English friends confuse me about cricket.'

'It did seem like there was quite a high proportion of Americans compared to British fans at the game,' says Nick. 'My colleagues and I were interviewed outside the stadium by some US TV channel. They were asking us if we understood the game. We explained: "Yes, we watch it every week!" Although to be honest it did seem like there were a lot of people who cheered loudest for the extra points, which in those days were pretty much automatic because they were so close to the goal posts. Looking back, it's clear the players were not as athletic as they are now, having seen NFL games in person in both eras. You can see why some people in the UK at the time thought the sport was simply big people hitting into each other.'

Despite the growing popularity of the sport in the UK, the NFL didn't play another game in the country until 1986 when the Super Bowl champion, Chicago Bears took on the Dallas Cowboys. By this time the NFL was not relying on British businessmen to put the game on, they were doing it themselves as part of an expanded international marketing plan. However, this three-year hiatus opened the door for another league to try its luck in the UK.

The USFL kicked off in March 1983 as a rival to the NFL. Owners of teams throughout the league's history included Donald Trump (future US president), Stephen Ross (future Miami Dolphins owner) and Edward J DeBartolo Sr (father of Edward J DeBartolo Jr, then owner of the San Francisco 49ers). It initially played its games in the spring, was in many NFL cities and had a TV deal with ABC and ESPN in the US. What it didn't have was a UK TV deal, although British American football magazines did give it some coverage. Less than a week after the Philadelphia Stars had beaten the Arizona Wranglers for the 1984 USFL championship in Tampa Stadium, the league played a 'postseason exhibition' at Wembley. On 21 July 1984 the Stars faced the Tampa Bay Bandits, a franchise part-owned by Hollywood star Burt Reynolds (who attended Florida State on a football scholarship), in a game broadcast live in the US on ESPN and played in front of about 20,000 spectators. Few people are aware the game even existed but it was an entertaining one and featured future Pro Football Hall of Fame enshrinee Sam Mills.

'I have no memory of how we found out about this game,' says Nick, 'but I do remember thinking: "Who are these two teams?" None of us had ever heard of them. It was a good game, though. The Bandits had a chance to take it to overtime when they were down 24-21, which is how it finished. We all wanted it to go to overtime so we could watch more. Everyone around us was shouting: "Bring on [English rugby's best kicker of the era] Dusty Hare!" Just like after the Global Cup game, we all went on to the pitch at the end. They were happy to allow it. You could just get on the field after the final whistle and talk to the players. It's quite different now of course.' UK fans might not have known about the USFL but they knew it was American football. And that in itself was a draw for a small group of people. Although the USFL eventually crashed and burned thanks to a foolhardy plan to move the schedule to the autumn, there was perhaps an opening in the UK they missed out on.

The 1985 USFL preseason ran from 2–17 February, with some of the games played outside the teams' base cities. There is an argument to be made that playing one of those games in London before the buzz of Super Bowl XIX on 20 January wore off could've placed the league firmly in the consciousness of a British public hungry for any sort of American football and the merchandise that went along with it. Certainly a missed opportunity.

By watching every week, and reading books by Nicky Horne, the host of Channel 4's coverage, or *Gridiron* magazine, Nick and others like him gradually learned more and more about the sport. 'I loved learning about the strategy and tactics,' says Nick, 'because many people at the time thought it was just about throwing the ball down the field as far as you could. Obviously it's a lot more than that but you had to really make the effort to seek out the information then and learn about it. That's why I still think a defensive game can be just as good as a high-scoring game.'

When the Premier League and its resulting TV coverage arrived, popping the NFL's already shrinking bubble in the UK, Nick was unaffected. Although his family were ardent Manchester United fans on the cusp of seeing their club become English champions for the first time in a generation, he had no interest in other sports. 'For soccer I was a Notts County supporter because that's where I went to university,' says Nick, 'but really it was just so people wouldn't talk to me about soccer. If they ask who you support and you say Notts County it just shuts the conversation down.'

As American football's popularity was dipping, Nick found himself working in the Netherlands, where coverage was nowhere near as good as it was in the UK. When the World League of American Football began in 1991, before a team was based in Amsterdam, Nick couldn't get to games. He ended up attending amateur leagues to get his fix.

Once he was back in the UK he was eager to see the London Monarchs and luckily he had a way to get in for free. 'My father-in-law at the time had a sign company that worked with the league for these games,' says Nick, 'so I would go along with him and pretend to put signs up. In return I would explain to him what was going on in the game. When I'd finished pretending to work we'd go to find some empty seats. We did this at White Hart Lane and at Stamford Bridge although once again I ended up sitting on some wooden planks because it was before they improved the stadiums.'

Nick has watched every Super Bowl since the NFL made its debut on UK screens, with the exception of Super Bowl XXXVII when he was based in China and the game kicked off at breakfast time. His years in the Netherlands certainly made him appreciate the coverage that UK fans had grown to love. 'One year it was meant to be shown on a particular Dutch channel but was switched at the last minute,' Nick says. 'It ended up being on a channel that was known for being cheap. The broadcast didn't have any ads so it just had a direct feed of the whole thing from the stadium. I don't think the commentators realised because you could hear them talking in the ad breaks, most memorably one of them asking: "Is this fucking mic working?" Oh, it certainly was.'

The hosts of the UK shows have been a lot better in Nick's eyes and he has a particular fondness for Mike Carlson. 'One time, after one of the games in London, I was travelling away from the stadium and I was faced with a packed train,' says Nick. 'Some people said: "Don't worry, we'll get you on," and they dragged me into the carriage. Next thing I knew I was right next to Mike Carlson. Later on in the journey, some guy next to me kept going on about the Packers and how cold it was in Green Bay. All he wanted to do was ask me if I knew how cold it was there. Eventually I said: "Look, when I get my season ticket I'll tell you." Mike enjoyed that and seemed to be the only one who got the joke I was making about the team's waiting list. I think Mike and Nat Coombs were the best NFL presenters we had in the UK because they explained everything. They talked through the Xs and Os to really get inside the game. The interaction between the two of them was fantastic as well, like it is with Osi Umenyiora and Jason Bell as they seem to be friends. Mike and Nat, Osi and J-Bell – you can tell they like each other. And that they're enjoying what they do.'

For many people the sport has simply been entertainment, but for Nick it was a vital distraction and a positive in his life when times were tough. He went through some dark days and knew he had to make a change in his life. Having the sport alongside him always helped. 'It's one of those things that even when things have been really difficult it's given me something to look forward to, such as attending the games in London,' says Nick. 'And even knowing I can watch the Packers every week on Game Pass has been a help. Sometimes I watch with a mate of mine. I retrained to become a yoga instructor – I wish I had discovered yoga when I was much younger – but he's got me beat because he then trained to be a priest.'

In his decades watching the sport, Nick has been able to see all 32 current franchises in person. However, it felt like he was going to get stuck on 31 and miss out on seeing his favourite team. 'My son lives in Florida and I was going over there to see him get married,' says Nick. 'Even better, that same week the Packers were playing in Tampa Bay against the Bucs.' It seemed like perfect timing. A family celebration, a trip to sunny Florida and the chance to finally watch the Packers play in the flesh – all in one week. 'Then Covid happened,' says Nick, 'and I couldn't leave the country.'

His plans were thwarted by the pandemic but luckily Nick only had to wait another couple of years to cross the 32nd team off his list. The Packers came to London on 9

October 2022, just a few weeks shy of the 40th anniversary of the first Channel 4 highlights show. It would finally give Nick a chance to see his beloved team and Aaron Rodgers, his favourite player of all time. (Yoga, says Nick, is one of the few things he has in common with Rodgers.)

It was no easy feat attending the game. Firstly, tickets were in exceptionally high demand. The combination of Tottenham Hotspur Stadium seating about 25,000 fewer fans than Wembley Stadium and the arrival of two teams in the Packers and New York Giants that are particularly well supported in the UK meant that many people missed out. Secondly, issues across the Transport for London network caused a chunk of fans to get to the stadium later than they had hoped. For many loyal Packers fans, seeing their team make their London debut (the final remaining team to do so) was like a religious experience. Nick's day was disrupted by actual religion, though. 'I missed the Packers' pre-game player introductions,' says Nick, 'because my friend who I went to the game with had to hold a church service earlier that day. The only reason we even made it in time for the national anthems was because we had been to the Vikings vs Saints game there the week before and learned from our travel mistakes. We arrived halfway through the first quarter for that particular game.'

Although Green Bay were upset by the underdog Giants it was still a special day for those fans who eventually got a chance to see their team, something that had been appreciated by fans of the other 31 franchises already. It's a bucket list event ticked off for Nick although he has high hopes of catching the Packers play a road game in Florida in the not-too-distant future. 'Until then,' he says, 'it's the usual routine of watching live every week, even if it means staying up until stupid o'clock so that I don't find out the score.'

Merchandise mania

ALTHOUGH HE'S a San Francisco 49ers fan, the Los Angeles Rams are a big part of why Dan Tearle developed a very special obsession. A family holiday to the US in 1981 – before Channel 4 was ever on air – included a stop in Southern California where he saw Anaheim Stadium (now called Angel Stadium), home of the Rams from 1980 to 1994. Dan remembers seeing Rams logos and merchandise but the sport this team actually played was a mystery.

Back in the UK, Channel 4 soon arrived and started broadcasting American football. Dan, who enjoyed many sports at the time, didn't pay any attention. This changed in the run-up to Super Bowl XX in January 1986 when NFL fever hit his school. Everyone seemed to be talking about American football and in particular the Chicago Bears. 'Bear-mania came around and everyone was a Bears fan at school,' he remembers.

Like many schoolkids of the time, Dan stayed up for some of the game and enjoyed it but within a week it was all forgotten. It would be eight months before another game arrived on TV and there was always something else to occupy his time. It took until 23 November 1986 for him to reacquaint himself with the sport. Channel 4 was showing week-old highlights of a Rams game at Anaheim Stadium in which the New England Patriots stormed back from a 12-point deficit in the fourth quarter to win 30-28. 'I couldn't take my eyes off it,' Dan says, 'and that's how it all started.'

While British sport felt rather grey in the 1980s, and soccer matches were marred by violence in stadiums, the NFL was a riot of colour – something that Dan, a keen artist, was well aware of. 'I loved the colour of it. Maybe it was that particular Rams vs Patriots game because visually it was a good uniform matchup. Compared with British sport it was a totally different experience. It was loud. It was colourful. It was far more exciting. That's what got me hooked. It wasn't the big hits. I think it was the presentation of it.'

Dan's favourite teams at this point were naturally the Rams and Patriots but that all changed while watching the playoffs. In the divisional round the New York Giants demolished the 49ers 49-3 and knocked Joe Montana out of the game with a concussion. While many of Dan's friends had gravitated towards the Bears a year earlier because it looked like they were set to dominate the league for years to come, Dan settled on the 49ers because he felt sorry for them and Montana. At the time he had no idea Montana had won a pair of Super Bowls in the previous six years, let alone that he would win another two in the next three years. 'I just felt so bad for them. Straight away, I thought: "This is going to be my team." I took an instant dislike to the Giants. Absolutely hated them.'

Family trips to the American Bowl games at Wembley followed, starting with the Rams' win over the Denver Broncos in August 1987. 'We were living in north London at the time, so we were close by,' Dan says. 'I'll never forget those American Bowls. They were just absolutely fantastic. It didn't matter that they were exhibition games, all the British fans were really appreciative.'

At soccer matches at Wembley, rival fans would need to be kept apart by lines of police officers and metal fencing. At the American Bowls, fans of all teams sat together. The rivalries were fun. The only animosity was towards those in the UK who sought to belittle American football. 'Everyone was so friendly. In the car park before the game people from all over the country were playing American football together for fun. I was too young to take part but I wanted to be around it. I'd never seen anything like that.'

As his love for the sport increased, so did his love for the aesthetics of the game. 'I started to draw players, just copying pictures from books and magazines,' says Dan. 'I used to draw the helmets so I could learn the logos. Because I was always drawing players and logos I got an eye for detail.' Meanwhile, Dan was amassing an impressive collection of American football magazines as publishers sought to cash in on the boom.

'I was consuming everything I could,' says Dan. 'I was doing a paper round back then and spent it all on NFL-related publications. The first book I got was a condensed version of the Marshall Cavendish part-work called simply *American Football*. The first issue of *Touchdown* magazine I got was the Super Bowl XXI preview edition.'

There is probably no one else in the world who has a better knowledge of the UK's American football magazines and books of the 1980s than Dan has. In his eyes, *Touchdown* magazine was the pinnacle. 'It definitely had better writers,' says Dan. 'Quite a few were American and it had British people such as Ken Thomas who was very knowledgeable. The magazine delved into statistics far more than the other UK magazines. It really taught you a lot. The magazine actually started off as a poster magazine for a few issues. It was just six pages with a big poster on the back. The first one was for the Vikings vs Cardinals preseason game at Wembley in 1983. It had a poster of the programme cover for that game painted by Chuck Ren.' If you grew up as a fan of the NFL in the UK in the 1980s you're almost certainly familiar with Ren's work whether you recognise the name or not.

Touchdown was not the only monthly magazine feeding the appetite of UK fans. '*Touchdown* had a lot more text than the other magazines but a lot fewer pictures and not as many colour pictures. *Gridiron* – originally called *Gridiron Pro* and no connection to the modern-day UK mag called *Gridiron* – tended to have colour but not quite as much in the way of text,' Dan recalls. 'The style of writing between the two was quite different. I used to buy *Gridiron* for the photos. *Gridiron* seemed quite trendy at the time, while *Touchdown* was very serious and highbrow. There wasn't much joking around in *Touchdown*. The college game got a lot more coverage in *Touchdown* too. When it was the draft, *Touchdown* was all over it. Looking back, because of its focus on facts and information I think *Touchdown* was the best one.

'However, back when I was a kid, I didn't like *Touchdown* as much precisely because it went a bit too deep for me. I bought *Gridiron* more frequently. There was a rivalry between the two magazines. There would be references in *Touchdown* to "lower quality publications", clearly meaning *Gridiron*. However, I think *Gridiron* covered Britball better than any of the other monthlies. I actually had some art published in *Gridiron* back in 1990, thanks to my dad, bless him. He arranged for me to send some drawings to them and they chose a Randy White piece that they put on the inside back cover. I still have the drawing too – they sent it back and, annoyingly, folded all my drawings in half.'

Although *Touchdown* and *Gridiron* were the 'big two' there was a third contender that didn't last as long as its more established rivals. '*Quarterback* was a really good magazine and quite underrated,' says Dan. 'It was pretty much a compilation of articles from the *Gameday* and *Pro* magazines [magazines produced as matchday programmes across the NFL], which we didn't get here. The articles were adapted and got new layouts. I found this out years later when I bought some old issues of *Gameday* and *Pro* and realised I'd already seen some of the features. Because of this they had a lot of good American writers but there were new bits added to cater to British fans.'

The most enduring UK publication covering the NFL in that era was not one of the monthlies though, it was *First Down*, a weekly newspaper that ran from 1986–2007. 'I didn't actually buy it for that long,' says Dan. 'When the weekly rival *American Football News* came out I found it better partly because it had more colour. *First Down* at the time seemed to focus on sensational stories. One of the first issues I saw as a kid was something about a team being full of drug addicts, and had these wild stories about what they were getting up to. It seemed to love a scandal but it also had great game reports. That's the main reason that I got it. It saw off *American Football News* pretty quickly and swallowed it up. To think we had three monthly magazines and two weekly newspapers for a while is insane. It cost me a fortune at the time.'

The British newspapers also made varying degrees of effort to cover the NFL. It seemed that the amount of coverage depended on whether someone in the office cared enough to suggest it. The *Daily Telegraph* has the best reputation from that era, going as far as to create its own magazine starting in November 1987, given away with the newspaper. These are now very hard to find. 'I've only got a couple of them at the moment,' says Dan. 'I've been trying to pick up a few. Like *Quarterback*, there was a lot of rehashed content from official NFL publications in America. At that point in my life, I was delivering papers rather than reading them but looking back I think the coverage was pretty good.

Other national newspapers went beyond printing the score too. The *Daily Express* published a book. There's a book from the *Daily Mirror*, but it was terrible.'

For a fan in the UK rather than the US, American football had to be sought out. While American fans in the 1980s were surrounded by the game and naturally took it for granted, British kids would have to make an effort. Colourful magazines such as *Touchdown*, *Gridiron* and *Quarterback* didn't just keep the British public up to date, they showed them how the game looked – a massive deal for such a visually arresting sport. Fans may stay for the sport's tactical battles, but they are drawn in by how the game looks. These magazines allowed fans to look at the sport whenever they wanted.

January 1987 saw a very welcome addition to the publishing landscape. For the first time the Super Bowl programme would be officially distributed in the UK. Dan was there from the start, scooping up the Super Bowl XXI programme and subsequent editions. These programmes created a much stronger connection between fans in the UK and the big game itself. 'Although XXI was the first one I got, the one for Super Bowl XXII was more special to me because it seemed to be the peak of NFL things being available over here,' he says. 'At that time it seemed like we could literally buy everything. I still have those Super Bowl programmes. They were not identical to the ones they sold in the US – they were thinner and the writing was adapted for the UK audience – but they were beautiful.'

The Super Bowl XXV programme was a very special version. To celebrate the championship's silver anniversary the NFL created a fold-out cover painted by Merv Corning, covering the history of the Super Bowl. It is pretty stunning but Dan, ever the artist, can't get over one error. 'There are so many details in there,' he says, 'it was just beautifully laid out. I absolutely love that one and Merv has been a big influence on me. But if you really look at it there's something wrong and I've got a little bone to pick with it. Merv Corning couldn't do facemasks. I'm sorry, but I've got to bring it up. On the 49ers helmet, the face mask starts too low and comes out too far. It's too angular. I loved all the little touches like the pin badges and stuff like that, and his reproductions of the magazine covers were absolutely perfect. A lovely painting. I feel very bad for picking on the facemask.'

As the 1990s went on, the NFL's popularity in the UK waned. After decades of domestic soccer seeming grey and unfriendly, the launch of the Premier League and Sky's coverage of the sport – following the feelgood factor generated by the 1990 World Cup in Italy – changed everyone's perception. (Of course, Sky's coverage and graphics were massively influenced by what American broadcasters had been doing with the NFL since the 1980s.) There was more live soccer on TV than ever before, with England's Premier League on pay TV joined by Italy's star-studded Serie A on Sunday afternoons on free-to-air Channel 4.

While the channel had once been known for its relatively unusual sports such as American football, sumo wrestling and kabaddi, it had now secured the rights to what was at the time the world's most glamorous domestic soccer competition. Serie A was the Premier League of its day. The schoolkids who at one time would have been obsessing over Eric Dickerson and Lawrence Taylor or the Chicago Bears and Miami Dolphins were now being drawn in by Gabriel Batistuta and Giuseppe Signori or AC Milan and Juventus. Although Channel 4 continued to show NFL highlights and the Super Bowl in the 1990s, the inevitable resurgence of soccer in the UK, coupled with the Italian league being the trendiest thing for British sports fans to watch, meant the NFL had lost its unique selling point. You were far more likely to see an Italian football shirt than an NFL jersey on a typical UK street.

'My interest waned a little bit,' admits Dan. 'It was around the time I met my wife, but more importantly a lot of the players that I had grown up with were getting to the end of their careers. It wasn't easy to warm to new players because they were replacing names we had known since the sport came to British TV. It was the end of a golden period for me. I kept an eye on things for a few years but I didn't watch it as much. Across the UK it seemed to wind down even though it never went away. There was a bit of a decline across the board. A lot of the magazines of the time disappeared and the merchandise wasn't as abundant.'

Crucially, the NFL decided to no longer play American Bowl games in the UK after 1993 with cities including Barcelona, Berlin, Tokyo and Sydney hosting the events instead. 'People in the UK got bored with the American Bowl,' says Dan. 'It was no longer a big thing, it was recognised as just a preseason game. No one cared about it being an exhibition game for the first few years.'

Not many copies of the early UK magazines, a vital element in connecting fans to the sport at a time when there was only a short weekly TV show, still survive. Luckily Dan has made it his mission to collect and preserve as many as possible. As the 1990s went on, his own enviable collection of UK magazines and books started to get smaller. Many were lost in various house moves, some sold on while he and his wife were living in a flat too small to contain his collection. In the 2000s Dan decided he wanted to rebuild that collection, acquiring all the issues that he had sold or misplaced as well as adding stuff he never had at the time.

'Half of my magazines have survived and I've owned them since they were new but obviously there are a lot I had to buy back again,' he says. 'There were also plenty that I had to replace because they were just worn out. Thankfully I've got more now than I had back then. I had a goal of putting the whole collection back together and made a point of collecting it all back again, which I did. The stuff I actually bought at the time seems a bit more special though.'

To create his new collection Dan devoted many hours to searching online as well as trawling charity shops and car boot sales for unwanted artefacts of that 1980s NFL craze. 'I would find a lot of British NFL stuff that people had got rid of because they lost interest,' says Dan. 'Back in the early 2000s it was very easy to find the things I wanted because American football had gone back to being incredibly niche. It was an easy collecting track to go on because nobody wanted it any more. It was so easy it felt like I was cheating. It's not like when I've been collecting Star Wars stuff.'

It's not just 1980s magazines and books that Dan obsesses over, it's pretty much anything the NFL licensed for sale in the UK. 'Everything was very much tailored to the British market and it was very carefully selected,' he says. 'We were lucky to get as much as we did. The NFL got it right by throwing all sorts of stuff at us. It kept us going. The jerseys, I've got some of them now, and they're terrible but they've got so much charm.' There can't have been any NFL fan growing up in the UK in the 1980s who didn't own or covet the officially licensed – but not wholly accurate – team jerseys, listed in ads as 'replica gameshirts'. Only a small selection of teams were available (49ers, Bears, Broncos, Cowboys, Dolphins, Giants, Jets, Oilers, Patriots, Raiders, Redskins, Rams, Seahawks and Steelers) and all followed a similar template: mesh jersey; team name on the front; no player name on the back; number of a star player on front, back and sleeves in a classic block font; NFL shield on sleeve. The Bears and Redskins were the only teams to get two different numbered versions with 35 replacing 34 on the Bears ones and 81 replacing 7 on the Redskins editions.

Meanwhile, only the Broncos and Redskins jerseys were white – even though the Cowboys and Dolphins generally wore white at home at this time while the Broncos did not. Dan has said that magazine ads at the time also referenced jerseys for the Falcons, Packers and an alternate white version for the Giants in text, but has seen no photographic evidence they were ever produced. 'The Bears jersey bothered me,' says Dan, 'because the team didn't wear block numbers. They stood out like a sore thumb to me. Back then it seemed like all NFL fans were consuming everything about the sport no matter what team an item was connected to. It was quite acceptable to wear, say, a Cowboys jersey one day and a Giants jersey the next. I don't think many people would do that nowadays but people like me became students of the whole league back then, no matter who your favourite team was.'

However, it was the magazines that had the most effect on Dan. The vivid and evocative photography in these vintage magazines, along with paintings by the likes of Merv Corning and Chuck Ren set Dan on an artistic path. 'Drawing NFL stuff has definitely been a constant in my life,' he says. 'In fact, it's probably the only thing that I've consistently done since the mid-1980s.'

Although Dan still creates NFL art for pleasure, he is also now doing it professionally and creating his own realistic style. 'I bought my first proper airbrush in the early 2010s,' he says, 'and it took me quite a long while to learn how to handle it. I went on a course in airbrushing about three or four years later and that completely changed my work. I've had a lot of commissions over the years including some pieces for the NFL office in London. They asked me to create a series of drawings – I don't know what they used them for but they paid me so it's up to them!'

Dan's work has become well known among the UK fan community but that's not to say that Americans aren't aware of his NFL art. In 2012 ahead of Super Bowl XLVI at Lucas Oil Stadium, some of his paintings went on display at the National Art Museum of Sport in Indianapolis. 'I've been able to sell my paintings worldwide; it's probably a 50-50 split between British buyers and Americans,' says Dan. 'It's kind of strange because plenty of American artists do it better than I do. When I sell an NFL painting it's usually somebody getting in touch with me saying what they want and I help them pick a suitable size. The price always depends on the complexity of the picture that they want. Nine times out of ten when they send me a photo they'd like it based on, it's too small for me to work from! It's nice when they want something from the 1980s and I can go back to them with options based on photos I like. Once I get started it usually takes three or four hours to draw the thing out. That's just the prep. When you factor in the actual painting itself it's about 20 hours of work to create one piece.'

It's a slow, methodical process because of Dan's obsession with detail. The sort of pictures he pored over as a youngster reading *Touchdown* and *Gridiron* brought to light little idiosyncrasies in uniforms that he is determined to replicate today. 'It takes a lot of time because I'm very fussy about my details, I want everything to be correct,' he admits. 'There's a lot of research that goes into it as well. Some other artists are talented but don't know the subject they're covering. There are nuances. I know what's right and what's not right. I pride myself on accuracy in that department.'

The famous Damac posters and framed pictures sold in the UK in the 1980s were a huge influence on Dan. 'This was my first introduction to NFL art – the posters and the wallpaper made up of the Damac pictures. I didn't know who painted them at the time. I was in love with them because they were so realistic, but still looked like paintings. It's sad that Chuck Ren, one of the main painters of the Damac products, passed away before the internet was widespread. If there's one person I would have loved to have spoken to it would have been him. I've been lucky enough to become good friends with his son Jon; he told me an awful lot of how they were done. Jon's a really good artist as well and he's done some NFL paintings too. It's hard to tell the difference between his work and his dad's because he was trained by Chuck and they work in the same style. Jon mostly paints wildlife now but I've spoken to him loads of times and he told me everything about his dad's NFL paintings.'

The Damac paintings were not always accurate, however. Notably, the Chicago Bears picture has a running back wearing 34 but to the keen-eyed observer it's obviously not Walter Payton – it's a picture of a running back for another team that has been changed. It's the sort of thing Dan noticed even back then. In recent years he has painted his own homage to this Bears picture, turning it into a Cincinnati Bengals version starring Louis Breeden.

'I've painted a lot of obscure players in my time because I've either liked the reference picture or I've liked the player myself, even if it wasn't a popular player,' says Dan. 'I think the most requested player I've painted is John Riggins. The interesting thing is that most of those commissions have come from British fans. I think there's a lot of old-school Washington fans who grew up with Riggins, and he was the

MVP of the first Super Bowl ever shown over here. That's surely not a coincidence.'

In fact, touchdown scorers that UK fans would see on Sunday afternoons on Channel 4 became a little bit of a speciality for Dan – although there's a more surprising name on his list. 'Eric Dickerson retweeted a painting I did of him. I've sent paintings off to Wesley Walker, Roger Craig and believe it or not, OJ Simpson.'

With Simpson retired from the NFL before Channel 4 even existed, a new British fan in the 1980s was unlikely to have watched many of his highlights. It's safe to say that 1988's *Naked Gun: From The Files Of Police Squad* was the first time he was widely seen by a UK audience. Of course he is now better known for his myriad legal issues but Dan, an NFL history buff, still wanted to paint him.

'It was a long time ago,' says Dan. 'At the time, I was on Facebook a lot and I messaged him. He was actually really nice to me. He was about to go to prison but I really wanted to paint him and send it to him. Obviously he wasn't going to give me his home address but he said he had a doctor friend in Arizona and asked if I could send it to him because he wasn't going to be around for a while. So I contacted his friend, made the arrangements and sent the painting off. But I didn't hear anything about it. I thought that was the end of the story but in 2021 the painting came up on eBay, and it included the letter that I sent with it. It was up for $2,000! I emailed the seller to say that I painted it and was just curious how he got hold of it. He replied saying he thought it was a fantastic painting and he acquired it from a house clearance. I don't know who bought it in the end but it was amazing to see it was still floating around.'

The less controversial figures who have ended up receiving a painting from Dan have shown their appreciation. 'All of them have been absolutely lovely,' says Dan. 'Wesley Walker was over the moon. He sent me some photos of him with the painting, and he posted out some autographed prints to say thank you. The Roger Craig story is a tragic one for me. He was in the UK for the International Series game at Wembley when the 49ers played the Broncos in 2010. He was flown over as one of the 49ers ambassadors and a friend of mine happened to know where he was staying. I got in touch with the NFL UK office and asked if I sent them a painting could they give it to him for me? They were really helpful and they made it happen.

'That day I was working a night shift. I got home the following morning and had a shower. When I came out of the shower I saw I had missed a phone call and I didn't recognise the number. I realised that whoever called me had left a voice message. It was Roger Craig telling me how much he liked the painting and that I'd really captured him. He told me he was going to be taking it back to the US with him. My favourite running back ever called me, I missed it and I was too scared to try to call him back. I just couldn't do it. So I left it at that. I did text him and he texted me back, so we exchanged a couple of messages but I missed out on speaking to him properly.' Not bad considering that when he was a child devoting hours to copying the pictures he saw in British NFL magazines, his parents said he should be drawing something 'that people might actually want to buy' when he was older. 'They changed their tune eventually,' Dan says, 'because I never stopped doing it. And I've done quite well. It's not about the money, it's about the satisfaction it has given me.'

Sundays are still all about the NFL with Dan, even though things have changed a lot since his favourite era. 'I still love American football, I just wouldn't place it on the same level as around 1987,' he says. 'The NFL of today does leave me a little bit cold sometimes. I think the game has changed. It's not got that old charm and it's very slick now. One of the things I loved when I got into the sport was looking at the uniforms – and realising uniforms were never really uniform. But now everything is almost perfect so it feels cold. I accept this is down to my age as much as anything, but when I watch the NFL now and I see a number on a jersey, I automatically pair it up to a player from my favourite era. Back in the day, I used to read so much. Just read, read, read. I would read depth charts, rosters, stats, everything. I could tell you pretty much all the starters from any team in any position. I couldn't do that today even though I've got more access to football now than ever. In the 1980s I would have to physically pull out a book or a magazine and sit down and read it. I don't buy magazines or anything like that any more, because everything's on the internet. I realised that if I can't be bothered to look on the internet for that information, I don't love it as much as I did, or at least I don't have the same physical interaction with the sport as I did.'

As well as a distaste for regular blockbuster trades compared with an era where you would usually associate a player with a single team for his entire career, Dan unsurprisingly has no time for the corporate blandness that has spread across the sport. 'Things have become so standardised that the Super Bowl logo is pretty much the same every year,' says Dan. 'It used to be much more visually appealing and there was a lot more imagination in it. We also got to a point where every Super Bowl half-time show is literally a mini concert with a big sponsor. A lot of Americans I know don't think of it like this because the sport has always been in their life. They probably don't focus as much on one decade or another, because it's been a constant. But British fans, those who stuck with the sport, have a strong focus on that time. It means more to us.'

The Monarchs are crowned – and dethroned

DURING THE 1980s people across the UK were adopting NFL teams as their own. It might be a star player, a cool-looking helmet or an amazing comeback win that sealed the deal, but no matter what it was, the connection was strong. If you were lucky enough to have other NFL-watching friends in your orbit, the chances are they liked different teams (although probably only the 14 teams the NFL were supporting through merchandise releases during that decade). The distance from the UK to any of these teams was massive, especially at a time when transatlantic plane travel was far less common than it is now and the world wide web hadn't even been invented. Fans connected with teams from watching Channel 4, buying merchandise and reading magazines. However, some people went beyond the NFL teams. They played for teams in the UK and were there for the birth of the country's first ever professional team.

'I remember when I got into the NFL like it was yesterday,' says James Hamlin. 'I was born in 1976 and I'd seen it on Channel 4 in the very early years but it never really caught fire for me. At that time on a Sunday there was nothing else worth watching on. It was just things like [religious shows such as the BBC's] *Songs of Praise* and [ITV's] *Highway*. In 1985 I was a little bit older and I was firmly into American stuff, like a lot of kids my age. It's how I started to get into hip hop back then, early stuff like electro and then Run-

DMC. But I was even into stupid stuff like *Dallas*, because it seemed so different. America felt very far away back then, not like now. Meanwhile there was barely any soccer on TV. So the 1985 season just hooked me and took me over the top. It was amazing. The hype leading up to Super Bowl XX was insane. I decided that whoever won the game was going to be my team.'

The fact that the NFL had arrived when televised sport was almost non-existent outside the Olympics and the men's soccer World Cup was hugely significant. ITV's head of sport John Bromley later said of this era: 'There was nothing else to watch in [soccer] terms and suddenly the Refrigerator was a bigger name than Gary Lineker; the Chicago Bears better known than Arsenal among the kids. Soccer made a big mistake – you must never go off the box.' But off the box it was and kids just like James were flocking to American football.

'The '85 Bears were so important in establishing the sport over here,' says James. 'They shot the league into the stratosphere. They had the "Super Bowl Shuffle" record out – which I bought and still have to this day – they had the video, they had the personalities and they were an amazing team to watch. Now I was off. I was absolutely obsessed from that particular point. It was as if the blue touchpaper had been lit all across the UK that night.'

Like many British schoolkids, James was bleary-eyed on the morning of Monday, 27 January 1986, but was energised by the fact he had found a new passion. 'In the UK at that time we were obsessed,' says James. 'We were like sharks looking for blood in the water. If you saw something you'd chase it down. I started to pick up bits of merchandise, like the VHS videos that came out covering the '85 Bears season, one was about the greatest quarterbacks, one about the best running backs, and *Crunch Time* about the hardest-hitting players in history. That started to build my world. I immersed myself in it, buying *Touchdown* and *Gridiron* magazines, the Pony NFL trainers, and the jerseys.'

As the viewing figures went up so did participation numbers. American football obsessives of all ages were forming teams up and down the country. A young James didn't want to be left out. 'I started playing when I was 11 or 12 years old,' he says. 'It seemed like loads of teams cropped up overnight. I joined a local team but I wasn't playing with kids my age, they were almost all quite a bit older because at the time over here there wasn't a version of the game for younger kids like me. I was a member of the Kingston Bengals and we used to play the famous teams of that era, such as the Crawley Raiders and London Olympians. Around this time *First Down* was giving almost as much coverage to British stuff as they did to American stuff. It was a great time and I would go to watch the London Ravens and the Olympians.

'I moved to the Heathrow Jets when I was about 13 or 14 and our head coach was a guy who used to play for the London Ravens. That's when it just took over my life. I was training five nights a week. I was still watching the games on Channel 4 but when you think about it, that only totalled about 40 minutes of highlights per show. This meant we as UK fans filled in the gaps ourselves. Ahead of the 1988 American Bowl at Wembley my team got a phone call from someone involved in the game saying they needed some lads to help do a half-time show with the San Francisco 49ers cheerleaders. I was too young to do it but my brother got to take part and I went with him. He had to dress up in a mascot outfit with the other boys. He had an Atlanta Falcon suit on and was with a 49ers cheerleader called Patti. I still have the signed photos of the cheerleaders we were given. Most importantly we got free tickets to the game. They were in the front two rows, which we thought was fantastic until we realised we had about 90 NFL players in front of us and we couldn't see a bloody thing.'

James was close to the field but a year later he would get much closer. 'The team I played for were pretty good and I was OK because I'd been playing since I was really young,' says James. 'We reached our championship game which was due to be played on the field at Wembley before the Philadelphia Eagles vs Cleveland Browns game. I ended up on American TV with [Browns linebacker] Clay Matthews and [Browns kicker] Matt Bahr for a show that I obviously never got to see. We were at a media day ahead of the game and got to meet big players including [Eagles running back] Keith Byers and [Eagles defensive end] Jerome Brown. We won our game and stayed to watch the American Bowl afterwards. And then we actually repeated and won the title again the next year. This time we played before the New Orleans Saints and Los Angeles Raiders. My brother, who played for a different team, was a ball boy at that American Bowl and he threw a game ball to me while I was in the crowd.'

As good as these days out at Wembley were, something even more significant was coming. The NFL fans in the UK were getting savvier and more discerning. Preseason exhibition games had been OK for a few years but the people buying tickets were becoming ever more aware that they were paying to see backups, many of whom would not be on an NFL roster come week one. 'You only saw the starters in the first series,' says James, 'and you never saw them again. So you might see Dan Marino take five snaps and that was it.'

The NFL wasn't blind to this problem. At one time simply having NFL teams play a game on British soil was enough. The star players would do lots of promo work and have their photos taken next to London landmarks. But eventually fans got bored of meaningless games. Luckily, the NFL had a plan.

Tex Schramm had been general manager of the Dallas Cowboys from their inception in 1960 until the team was bought by Jerry Jones in 1989. When he left the Cowboys he started the ball rolling on the World League of American Football, although his plan wasn't to have it under the NFL umbrella. 'My vision was for an independent, major international league which would be strong enough to stand on its own feet,' Schramm told South Florida newspaper the *Sun-Sentinel* in October 1990. 'The desire of those who have a different vision is, quite obviously, for a smaller league, more closely attached to the NFL.'

The league would end up being overseen by the NFL and used to develop players and grow the game outside the US. The initial plan was for ten teams, with three outside North America. London was the eighth city to be awarded a franchise, taking the final European slot after Frankfurt and Barcelona had offers accepted first. Now all the NFL had to do was persuade fans in the UK it was worth buying tickets for games where even the best players weren't able to stick around on NFL rosters. At least these would be competitive games.

'Capital Radio was pushing it all the time,' says James. 'They wanted to get people in the stadium by fair means or foul. There were lots of ticket giveaways. I went to the first game and I'm pretty sure we got those tickets for free.' To increase visibility there were live WLAF games on now-defunct satellite channel Screensport (at a time when very few people had satellite or cable TV) but crucially there was a Saturday morning highlights show on Channel 4 that focused on the London Monarchs. A key part of the show was future Sky Sports legend Jeff Stelling going behind the scenes and spending time with the players. 'That show was so good because Channel 4 had so much access,' says James. 'It was like reality TV before that was a thing. It was what kids like me were crying out for. It spiralled from there and became an absolutely amazing time to be a fan.'

Wembley Stadium was a big venue and it was hard to get it anywhere near full for WLAF games. However, even the lowest crowds of around 35,000 for Monarchs home games were more than almost every soccer team in the UK at that time. The only soccer club that topped the Monarchs' average of about 40,000 spectators per game in 1991 was Manchester United.

'It was all about the atmosphere at Monarchs games,' says James. "All Right Now" by Free was the song they used to play in the stadium when the Monarchs scored a touchdown. When you talk to people who were there they'll tell you the crowd felt like 80,000. We felt part of something special. It wasn't like Wembley is now where they have soccer's FA Cup semi-finals and so many other games and events there. The old Wembley still had a sense of magic. You didn't get to go there very often. I went to a couple of soccer matches when I was a kid, but because I was American football-focused, I was never really that bothered. Kids didn't go to many soccer matches back then because it was violent. Monarchs games were different. There was music, energy and fun. And it didn't matter that you didn't know who the players were at first because the TV show would follow them on road trips and you connected with the team. They really upped the merch game too. You could go to a game, buy merch and it wasn't too expensive.'

Another thing that helps people bond with a new team is winning. The Monarchs did a lot of that, starting the season

9-0 before losing the regular season finale to the Barcelona Dragons, who they would later destroy in the first ever World Bowl. 'They were winning,' says James, 'and they were winning with swagger. Everything was about entertainment. There were lots of touchdown dances and they were allowed to have personalities. It was around this time I started taking less of an interest in the Bears. They had become so boring to watch. Meanwhile, the Monarchs had a great offense, a tough defense, everything was imaginative – and I was seeing it in person.'

The first season was a great success for the Monarchs although teams in North America struggled to win games or attract fans. The WLAF's second season was a disappointing one for the London team. They lost a lot of close games and finished nowhere near the playoffs. 'Fans had got to know all these players for the Monarchs and then after winning the World Bowl many of the stars were gone,' says James. These included fan favourites such as Jon Horton, Roy Hart, Andre Riley, Steve Gabbard, Dana Brinson and Mike Renna, along with head coach Larry Kennan, who became the Seattle Seahawks' offensive coordinator. Not long after the Sacramento Surge beat the Orlando Thunder in World Bowl '92 at Montreal's Olympic Stadium, the NFL closed the WLAF. James, like many other American football fans – but especially those who had become attached to the Monarchs – became disillusioned with the sport. 'From 1992 to 1995, those are the lost years for fans of the sport in this country,' says James. 'When the WLAF closed in 1992 I moved on. I was 16 going on 17 and every spare penny I could get my hands on was spent on CDs. I remember thinking the closure was a shame, but I understood why they did it.'

There were changes happening in James's life and in the wider world that started to relegate the NFL on people's list of priorities. 'In 1992 I was heavily into hip hop,' says James. 'That year my mum came home and said we were getting satellite TV in time for the Cricket World Cup on Sky. This meant I had access to *Yo! MTV Raps*. I would come home from college at 5pm, get the video set up ready to press record and pause because you didn't know what songs were going to come on the show. I stopped playing American football around this time, too – playing it was not what people did at this point. I had become 100 per cent into hip hop.'

American football had been a mainstay of youth culture in the UK for a few years. James had been thrilled to see characters on *Grange Hill* wearing NFL jerseys, a sure sign that kids across the nation were on board. Hip hop was also getting bigger at this time, not just for James, but for many other young people in the UK. While hip hop was only getting cooler, the NFL was losing its cool factor rapidly. It would soon lose its title of the coolest US sporting import to a game with much closer ties to hip hop. 'By the end of 1992 American football wasn't cool,' says James. 'It was starting to get very nerdy. At the opposite end of this was the Barcelona Olympics and the basketball Dream Team. That was like something from another dimension. It was peak Michael Jordan.' As famous as NFL players had been in the UK, few were as recognisable or as marketable as Jordan. Despite a relative lack of basketball on TV, the clothes, music, attitude and accessibility of playing the game made the NBA a much hotter property in the UK than the NFL was. Despite this, the NBA was never able to come close to matching the NFL's 1980s popularity.

In 1995 the London Monarchs and the WLAF returned. This time it was based entirely in Europe and the Scottish Claymores, were added to the league. For those who were kids when the NFL was new on Channel 4, the timing wasn't great. 'I was 19 when the WLAF returned and many games were on early Saturday evening,' says James. 'Like many people my age, I was unlikely to stay in to watch them. I had other things to do. I followed what was going on though and it was interesting to see the likes of Brad Johnson with the Monarchs. I would only watch occasionally. You'd see the small crowds at White Hart Lane and it felt like they were chasing something from 1991 they would never reach again. When I think back to Monarchs games I can still hear Free playing in my head. They could never replicate that.'

James's interest in the sport was rekindled in an unexpected place. 'I went off to university in Derby in 1996,' he says. 'To my surprise, they had an American football team at the university so I decided to start playing again. Because I had played loads, I was pretty good.' It fired his enthusiasm for the game again although he still found the WLAF unappealing. That same year England hosted the Euro '96 soccer tournament and reached the semi-finals. After failing to qualify for the 1994 World Cup and exiting Euro '92 without a single win, England's national team had captured the imagination of the public following six dismal years of disappointment. The St George's Cross had become a strong piece of branding during the tournament, and English identity – rather than British identity – was coming to the fore for English people. By 1998 the WLAF had become NFL Europe and the London Monarchs had become the England Monarchs – with the St George's Cross prominent on the new logo. The team had moved on from Wembley, White Hart Lane and Stamford Bridge and were travelling to much smaller stadiums around the country. The crowds were also shrinking. 'I was involved in an all-star game in 1998 which was played at Crystal Palace National Sports Centre before a Monarchs game,' says James. 'There was basically no one there. Nobody even cared. When they became the England Monarchs that really was the end.'

It wasn't the end of James's love for the NFL though. It just happened to take a while to become a big deal for him again. 'In 2012 I properly got back into it,' he says. 'I was soon doing an American football podcast, I was putting on Super Bowl parties, I was meeting players at press events. I was also working in ticketing at the time so I saw another side of the business of sport. It was a different type of fandom to the one I had when I was younger. I never thought it would be possible to put on a Super Bowl party with 5,000 people or having guests such as [former Rams wide receiver] Torry Holt over to take part. We got people including Mike Carlson and all these other guys on our podcast and that was amazing. I would say that my fandom was maybe bigger than it was in my younger days. It was cool to get a second bite of the cherry. I still watch the NFL religiously. Nowadays it has a more exciting offseason than it ever had and that's by design.'

James's consumption of the sport is rather unusual though. Where more fans keep a focus on their favourite team, he likes to cast his net wider. 'I had been obsessed with the Bears,' says James. 'I used to get team yearbooks and know everything about every player. Then they got boring. That was the hard thing. They weren't losing shootouts. They were hard to root for. I did get into soccer but I'm not really into that very much any more. I've got three kids under six so that takes up a lot of time. I'm a Tottenham Hotspur fan and it just seems like they always have an awkward kick-off time and end up losing to teams they shouldn't lose against. It used to put a black cloud on my weekend. So now I don't just follow a team. I follow the narrative. I don't need the headaches in my life. I never got into college football. Let's say I was a Notre Dame fan, what am I going to do after a big win, go out on my road and start celebrating with people who've never even heard of the team? I'm also off basketball now. I think all the player empowerment stuff is awful. So in the end, I'm happy for the Bears to win, but I can't use up mental energy on a team.'

John Madden Football
coaches British gamers

WHEN ELECTRONIC Arts [EA] founder Trip Hawkins asked legendary broadcaster and former NFL head coach John Madden to lend his name to a new American football game in 1984 he was planning, Madden was on board under one condition: that the game was realistic. This was a challenge with the technology of the 1980s. There had been American football video games released that had proved quite popular such as Irem's arcade game *10-Yard Fight* (which was adapted for the Nintendo Entertainment System [NES] when the console was launched in the US), Atari's trackball-based arcade hit *Football* and Mattel's *NFL Football* for the Intellivision and Atari 2600 home consoles. None of them were remotely realistic, however.

Madden not only wanted 11 players from each team on the field – something other games hadn't been able to pull off – he hoped the game would become a way to teach and test plays. At a time when computer games were generally produced quickly and cheaply, Hawkins' game was coming along very slowly and costing a relative fortune. Eventually in 1988, four years after the game was conceived, *John Madden Football* was released for the Apple II computer. It was complicated, realistic and very slow. In 1989 another flawed computer game version of the sport was released: *ABC Monday Night Football*. The creators of that game, Park Place Productions, caught the eye of EA who approached them about making a new version of *John Madden Football* for a console.

In 1990 EA released *John Madden Football* for the 16-bit Sega Genesis (known as the Sega Mega Drive outside North America), with the game quickly becoming a critical and commercial hit. For US console gamers who had been playing the simplistic *Tecmo Bowl* on the 8-bit NES, this was a stunning upgrade if they could afford the more powerful hardware.

The Mega Drive was released in the UK in September 1990, more than a year after the Genesis arrived in the US. Despite interest in the NFL starting to wane in the UK, EA decided to release the game here just ahead of Christmas in 1990. It was far from the first American football game to come out in the UK but it was the first one to achieve widespread acclaim from magazine reviewers. *Mean Machines*, the most influential UK console magazine of the time, put the game on the cover, described it as the best release for the Mega Drive so far and praised it for being 'highly addictive and technically stunning'. If you will pardon the pun, it was a game-changer for the UK. Although it may have helped US fans learn more about the nuances of playbooks and strategy, for many UK novices it was like a playable tutorial for a sport they didn't previously understand. Encouraged by gushing reviews, plenty of UK Mega Drive owners with no knowledge of the sport picked up the game to see what the fuss was about. As the years went on its influence became clear.

Many of these gamers were kids at the time, exposed to the sport's nuances for the first time. Among these was Grant Sales. 'My first memory of the NFL was being aware of Dan Marino in the late 1980s,' he says. 'It felt to me that Marino was the first player to get into the British consciousness. As a kid I got a jersey from a supermarket that was clearly meant

JOHN MADDEN FOOTBALL COACHES BRITISH GAMERS

to look like a Marino Dolphins jersey. It was the right colour
and texture with a number 13 but it wasn't officially licensed.'

Grant didn't pay much attention beyond that. He wasn't
making plans to watch highlights on Channel 4 each Sunday
or heading to the corner shop to buy *First Down* every
Thursday. He was more interested in his Mega Drive. In
the early 1990s he got *EA Sports Double Header*, a bargain
two-in-one cartridge with a pair of EA's biggest hits. One
was *EA Hockey*, which featured international ice hockey
teams (the US version, *NHL Hockey*, had real pro teams),
a surprise hit in the UK. The other game was *John Madden
Football*. There was no NFL licence so the 16 teams in the
game were simply named after a city or region. (*Madden NFL
94* was the first to feature official team names and logos; a
year later player names were also included.) 'That first game
was one you could constantly enjoy playing,' says Grant. 'It
was never so hard that you felt you were never going to win
a championship. And it was never too complicated. These
days, we have to press about seven buttons to do anything.'

In the 1990s a new video game cost about £40, which
means that taking inflation into account they cost about
£80 in 2023's money. The average age of a gamer was also
considerably lower than it is now, meaning acquiring new
games was not a regular occurence. A kid in the UK was
unlikely to get each new annual iteration of the *Madden* series.
Luckily Grant had friends who had also become addicted to
the game. 'A friend of mine got *John Madden Football '92*
and it became a big thing for me and my mates,' says Grant.
'We'd all go to play it at someone's house on weekends or after
school. That was where I really started to get into it – because
I wanted to beat my mates.'

Sports games bring out that competitive edge in friends
and Grant decided he would go the extra mile so he could

become the best at it. 'I started to read more about the sport,' he says. 'I'd go to the library to get books out so I could read up on, say, what running plays coaches would call at certain times. For a lot of my friends they would simply play in the shotgun the entire time, usually calling a Hail Mary no matter the circumstances. No one really understood playing defense. The 3-4 and 4-3 meant nothing – all we knew was blitz, blitz, blitz. I figured out when my friends would expect me to pass or run so I would throw in a bit of play action. I'm not the best at pressing buttons to spin, jump, dive or anything like that. So my focus was confusing my mates with play action. I soon started to be the best player because I had made a point of learning more about the sport. They soon got wise to this and wanted to put me at a disadvantage. The handicap was that they were allowed to pick the best teams in the game and I could only choose bad teams. That's how I settled on Green Bay [who were not included in the Mega Drive's first *John Madden Football*] because in that version of the game Brett Favre wasn't on the roster yet, it was Don Majkowski at that point. So I had the Packers because they didn't have a very good quarterback. Otherwise I was going to gravitate towards Dan Marino or Joe Montana.'

The Packers would eventually end up with back-to-back first ballot Hall of Famers at the position but that was no use to Grant. 'I would tell my friends: "I can even beat you with a bad quarterback", that sort of thing,' says Grant. 'I could just pick them apart because I knew what I was doing. The following year I got to play *John Madden Football '93*. Obviously the series only had numbers for players at the time so I had no idea why the Green Bay quarterback was now "4" rather than "7". Eventually I started watching the sport, discovered it was Favre and absolutely fell in love with the gunslinger. At this point the games convinced me to watch on TV, which helped me become an even better player. My friends and I carried on playing against each other for many years. We wouldn't have been interested in the NFL without the *Madden* games. You may enjoy, say, a 66-yard touchdown through the air in *Madden* but it looks even better in real life. Which meant I got even more excitement out of doing it in the game because I was seeing spectacular plays from NFL coverage on TV.'

The game fed Grant's knowledge of the sport, which in turn helped him learn more about the game. 'When I started, the Hail Mary was my main play,' he says, 'so when I saw a team running that in the highlights on TV I was thrilled because I spotted it before the snap. You feel very proud of yourself at that point. Then I would identify a play action from the way the running back was moving. Next I could see when a defense was showing blitz. I would then figure out what I was up against in *Madden* and react accordingly. The more I saw on TV the more I could put into *Madden*.'

Grant got deeper into the sport and deeper into its associated video games. At the end of 1993, EA brought out an extra game that would have only a very small audience in the UK. 'Then I got to play *Bill Walsh College Football* on the Mega Drive,' says Grant. 'It got me into college football as well as the NFL. Although I certainly preferred *Madden* to the *Bill Walsh* games.' Only the first Bill Walsh game was released in the UK, with follow-up *Bill Walsh College Football '95* a North American exclusive. Although that was the final game to bear the legendary coach's name, EA released college football games every year until 2013 (but never in the UK) when legal issues surrounding the use of player likenesses became so prominent the series was mothballed. EA has announced it will revive the series in 2024.

THE AMERICAN FOOTBALL REVOLUTION

Life was progressing for Grant, and as much as he loved the *Madden* series there were things that got in the way. 'When girls came on the scene,' says Grant, 'my friends and I couldn't find as much time to get together to play against one another. We would still play on our own and I used to play a lot – whenever I had nothing else to do I was on *Madden*. Things then changed a lot for me because I joined the military. It was a while before I played much of *Madden* again.'

During his stint in the military Grant didn't get to enjoy much in the way of console gaming and his NFL viewing was confined to Freeview with no Sky Sports available. 'I didn't have a lot of internet access either,' says Grant. 'I kept up with the Packers as best I could, partly thanks to email bulletins. And I got to see the NFL on Channel 5's late-night broadcasts. I could watch those games if I was working a night shift. I would usually say to someone: "Look, you go off and do this, I'll watch the game and then I'll go and do the rest of the checks." At the end of all this I ended up with an Xbox. I thought: "Right, let's see how *Madden* is looking nowadays." My reaction was "wow" because the graphics were a quantum leap over what I'd been used to. [Packers wide receiver] Greg Jennings actually looked like Greg Jennings rather than just six pixels on top of each other. More importantly, the depth of the single-player game had taken a huge leap. You could see formations move as they should, for example. The game required more thought than it did in the earlier editions. It was very much a progression, which was ideal for those of us who had started to understand the game better as the series developed. It was a more advanced *Madden* for my more advanced understanding of the sport.'

With Grant now able to finally devote time to the game again, he found himself in a golden era. '*Madden 2005* and

Madden 2006 were the last real single-player-focused ones,' he says. 'They were the absolute pinnacle for me.'

Change was on the horizon for the *Madden* series though, and it wasn't the evolution that Grant wanted. 'I was buying the new *Madden* game each year,' he says, 'but as time has gone on I've been enjoying it less. They've made the game much more about Ultimate Team [an online mode where players buy digital trading cards of players to fill out their roster] and have neglected the traditional single-player mode. I like playing against my friends but I have no interest in playing online. I'm just not that bothered about getting really good at it. I'm not interested in sitting down to play online only to get destroyed by someone who's sat there playing it every hour for the past six days. There's no fun in that. If I play with my friends it's just for fun. No one gets too annoyed if they lose and no one gets too happy if they win. It's just a good laugh. Ultimate Team made it too serious, too competitive. It used to be guaranteed fun for me no matter what I did.

'Nowadays EA does a thing called EA Play where for £20 a year you can have a ten-hour trial of the newest games. That's enough for me these days. The only new online thing I enjoy is where you coach your team rather than control the players. With that it doesn't matter how long you've spent on it. You know if you haven't traded for a certain player or picked the right free agent then that's your fault. It doesn't come down to how much time you've played and practised. It comes down to the knowledge of the game and how much you've learned from watching and studying. During those trials I tend to play the story mode until my ten hours are done. The single-player offline story mode doesn't make them any money, unlike selling Ultimate Team cards, so the story is done in about seven hours.'

No one, not even Trip Hawkins, could have predicted that the *Madden* series of games would become such a phenomenon. The *FIFA* series of soccer games (now called *EA FC*) have been more commercially successful around the world obviously, but the importance *Madden* games had on promoting the NFL outside North America cannot be matched by the equivalent soccer series. The *Madden* series became a teacher to curious gamers who needed to learn the rules. It became a coach to those fans who had a rudimentary understanding of how the sport was played but wanted to grasp the nuances. It even became a precursor to NFL Game Pass in the decades before anyone could've imagined a year-round, on-demand streaming platform. If you didn't have VHS tapes filled with Super Bowls or regular season highlights and games you'd recorded from TV, this was your only chance to get the NFL on your screens in the offseason.

It was *Madden* that made him a Packers fan and for Grant the two things are forever connected. 'I never pick another team,' says Grant. 'I will never be a team other than Green Bay. I just want to go deep into playing as that team. I hate the idea of playing as another team against the Packers. I love all the American sports and I'm a fan of the St Louis Blues in the NHL and the Minnesota Timberwolves in the NBA but I don't feel the need to only play as them in video games. At the end of the day, it's just playing. I don't ever feel it's just playing when I'm controlling the Packers in a *Madden* game. If I'm playing as another team I'm not helping Green Bay. If I choose another team and win the Super Bowl in the game as them that means the Packers haven't won it so I can't maintain my interest. Once I was involved in an online league and we got to "draft" the teams we would control. But like the real NFL there was only one of each team and because I got to the draft late I missed out on the Packers.

So I did my best through the course of the season but when it came to me playing against the person who picked Green Bay I just quit as soon as it started so the Packers got the win by default. I just couldn't play against them or it would feel like I let the Packers down. When I was younger I read about the 1985 Bears because they started putting historic teams in those early *Madden* games. I played against them and it was so hard. I thought: "This is not good." So I turned it down to the lowest difficulty and beat them 56-0. Probably once a week I would put it on easy mode just to smash the Bears.'

NFL style lights up a dark time

WHILE THE 1980s had been a boom time for the NFL in the UK, with merchandise made for the market flying off the shelves, the 1990s was a different time. American football was no longer the cool new sport. Although plenty of people had stuck with the game, many more had considered it to be a fad they had grown out of.

It was hard for the NFL to stay relevant among the British youth. The Premier League and Italy's Serie A had helped British kids fall in love with soccer without dealing with the ghosts of stadium violence from the 1970s and 1980s. Meanwhile, Michael Jordan, and his Nike line of shoes and apparel had started to create a market for basketball in the UK ahead of the 1992 Olympics and the Dream Team's debut. Jordan and the Chicago Bulls became global fashion brands in effect and helped along all the other North American teams and leagues with them. American NFL fashion clothing – quite distinct from the stuff made for the British audience – helped keep the sport and its teams in the minds of young people across the UK.

Chris Milner wasn't much of an NFL fan in this era but his career is now dominated by it. 'The first time I can remember noticing the NFL was in the early days on Channel 4,' he says. 'I was about ten years old and I couldn't sleep so I went downstairs and my dad was watching it. He watched it a lot but I didn't get into it like he did.'

It took a couple of decades for Chris to gain an appreciation for the game and it didn't even happen in the UK, although he can thank his dad for steering him in the right direction. 'Cut forward 20 years later and I had moved to Washington DC,' says Chris. 'My dad said: "I don't know if you remember this, but we used to watch American football on Channel 4. And one of the teams that were good at the time was the Washington Redskins. If you're going to Washington and you get into American football, you should support your home team." And so I did. I went to Washington, I lived there for seven years and followed the Redskins avidly. Much to my chagrin and detriment.'

Chris had missed out on a glorious period for the franchise when they had won three of the first ten Super Bowls shown live in the UK. This success had ensured they were clearly one of the most popular teams among UK fans. It had been slim pickings since then. 'I arrived two years before RG3 [Robert Griffin III] was drafted,' says James. 'I got to experience bad Redskins football: John Beck and Rex Grossman. Santana Moss and London Fletcher felt like the only bright spots on the team. Then for one year, it was the greatest season to be in DC as a football fan ever. There was an insane high during RG3's rookie season. And it's been basically downhill from there, and that's without even mentioning the scandals. It's not been a great team to follow.'

Most British fans of American football don't get the experience Chris had of developing a love for the NFL while being immersed in it and getting to see live games. So despite his team struggling most of the time, Chris had a blast. 'I always tried to get to as many games as I could,' he says. 'I got to see RG3's rookie record-setting touchdown run against Minnesota live. It was one of the greatest experiences of my life. My first friend that I made in DC is still in a fantasy league with me. He is a diehard Washingtonian and he helped me get into the team. Playing fantasy football with him gave me a greater appreciation for the league in general, rather than just a specific team, because fantasy forces you to do that. I just fell in love with the NFL.'

The plan had been for Chris to stay in DC indefinitely but like many plans it just didn't work out. 'I wasn't planning on coming back so I didn't have any support system in the UK beyond my family,' he admits. 'I came back during the 2017 season and I was desperately looking for places to watch NFL games or people to watch it with. In America, it's easy: you go to the closest bar and find people to hang out and watch a game with. I took for granted how much I enjoyed doing that.'

The UK landscape was totally different. Now people who Chris might have considered enemies in DC were ideal friends. 'A few months after I came back to the UK the Super Bowl rolled around,' says Chris. 'So I looked for somewhere to watch the game and the closest venue to me was a barbecue place. I thought: "Fine, I'll go there. At least I'll be around people." So I turned up in Washington gear and straight away saw three guys standing at the bar. One in Giants gear, one in Cowboys gear, and one in Eagles gear. I just walked up to them and said: "Looks like we need a fourth, guys." We had an NFC East full house. It turned out they were all Americans who were annoyed they'd been sent to London to work which meant they had to watch the Super Bowl really late at night. I ended up latching on to them and we got absolutely hammered. The Eagles won the Super Bowl that night so it was very special for one of them. It ended up being one of the greatest bonding nights of NFL fandom ever. It just happened to be with Americans in a bar in London.'

Thankfully for Chris, the NFL UK community was ready to save the day and give him more than just one good night out. 'I went to a meet-up arranged by NFL Girl UK

NFL STYLE LIGHTS UP A DARK TIME

[Liz Bhandari] where I met Hugh Coles,' says Chris, 'who had just started a business called National Vintage League [NVL], which was selling vintage NFL clothing in the UK, and we got on very well. At first it was just a little pop-up shop and I started helping him sell stuff. Then I was looking for a job and he said he needed help with NVL because it had become too big for him to do out of his house any more. By mid-2018 we were properly working together and grew the business exponentially to the point where it is today.' Chris is now running NVL himself, however. Hugh left the business in June 2021 with Chris's blessing to concentrate on his successful acting career.

Most British fans of the NFL get into the sport because they already have some fans around them who help get them interested. Chris was the exact opposite. He was a hardcore fan desperately looking for people like him. Thanks to the community in the UK, he not only found those fans, he found a sense of belonging and a job he was passionate about.

'When I arrived back in the UK I wanted a career in the sport,' says Chris. 'I wanted to write articles initially. When I met Hugh for the first time he asked me what my goal was over here. I told him I wanted to be a commentator or reporter at the first ever UK Super Bowl. This made people laugh but I told them I thought it could happen. I think eventually there will be a Super Bowl here so there's a chance that I could be able to fulfil the prophecy.'

Time will tell whether Chris is proved correct on that point but what is beyond doubt is that he's played a huge part in keeping alive the merchandise that helped the NFL maintain a foothold with a British audience beyond just the hardcore viewers. Fashion was vital to ensuring the NFL's teams and logos didn't vanish when the fad ended. However, the first goal of NVL was making sure UK fans didn't get scammed. 'We were basically trying to combat the large amount of fakes sold on the internet because we could see fans getting ripped off over here,' says Chris. 'There are Chinese companies that are very skilled in creating fakes so we wanted to be able to give UK fans the opportunity to get authentic jerseys for their favourite teams. And at the same time we wanted to help the environment. Buying vintage items rather than buying new jerseys is a lot more sustainable and lets you keep stuff out of landfill while supporting your team. I've never really seen the point in spending £300 on a new jacket when you could get ten second-hand jackets for that – and they'd probably be much cooler and have a history.'

The goals are admirable but would've come to nothing if British fans were only interested in current stars. However, Chris soon realised there was a massive appetite in the UK for clothes and players from the past. 'Most people who love the NFL know that the history is one of the most important aspects of it,' he says. 'You can go back to say 10 or 20 years before and unwrap a jersey from a player who was a beast back then. For many fans that's a cooler thing than getting the most recent jersey of a player who may be off the team pretty soon. Why pick them when you can pick a legend? Our customers are fans looking to celebrate their teams and the history of the game – but also wanting that vintage look because it's much cooler.'

Not every fan is going to notice but the manufacturers selling NFL apparel in the 1990s were very different to the ones today. In 2000 Reebok signed a ten-year deal with the NFL that from 2002 gave them the exclusive rights to make the Pro Line apparel that players and coaches wear. Up until that point brands including Starter, Nike, Puma, Adidas, Wilson, Champion, Apex One, Pro Player and Logo Athletic had all been seen on the field and sidelines. A decade later

Nike took over from Reebok, although New Era became the hat supplier to the league. 'The thing is, the stuff from the 1990s was made to last,' says Chris. 'It was the best stuff. The companies were making high-quality garments and competing with each other. This means clothes are still perfectly viable today, because they were made so well back then. When there's an exclusive deal there's no incentive for them to make truly high-quality stuff. What's the point? You have no competition. NVL was perfect for me because I have a love for the sport and for the older fashions. The 1990s was a crazy cool time for statement pieces of fashion. There was a pop culture boom in that decade: MTV, the Chicago Bulls, hip hop … American culture in general was at an apex. And that filtered over to the UK so things that were cool in the US became cool here. It became a perfect storm of sports clothing, pop culture, hip hop and TV. The result was that a lot of people have an affinity with that era even if they are too young to remember it.'

The clothing produced for NFL teams in the 1990s made a huge impact in the fashion stakes in the US and that inevitably trickled down to the UK. 'At NVL we source 99 per cent of our stock from inside of the UK,' says Chris. 'What's amazing is we have people in America buying from us. We've been told things like: "I'm in Oregon and I can't get this sort of stuff." We've had NFL players reaching out to us to get stuff when they move teams because we've become the best option.'

The era that most of NVL's stock comes from has certainly struck a chord with fans in the UK, especially those who grew up watching the sport for the first time in the 1980s and 1990s. 'There are a lot of NFL fans who want to talk about the history of the sport, the cool things, the cool jerseys, the cool stories, the stuff in the past,' says Chris.

'People get really nostalgic about the NFL but especially what are arguably the two greatest decades in terms of NFL storylines – the 1980s and 1990s. And newer fans have got into that as well, so now some of them are out wearing vintage items of NFL clothing that are older than they are.'

When it comes to NFL fashion of this era one brand in particular stands out and that's Starter. No other company seemed to understand what the public wanted from sports merchandise better. Its iconic jackets became must-have items in America and soon became popular on British streets.

'Starter is the be-all and end-all when it comes to NFL clothing that crossed over into cultural relevance on both sides of the Atlantic,' says Chris. 'The company was founded in 1971 in New Haven, Connecticut by David Beckman. He started with baseball, but after years of getting turned down, he eventually managed to sign a deal with the NFL to be a sideline apparel brand. At the same time, hip hop was coming up in the US, first in New York, and then other major cities such as LA. His son Brad married Paula Abdul and had connections throughout the music industry. Brad knew Will Smith in his *Fresh Prince of Bel Air* days so he wore a lot of Starter on the show. Then DJ Jazzy Jeff appeared in a Starter ad. Soon Run-DMC were wearing Starter jackets on stage. Before long Starter jackets weren't just about sports. They were about being cool.'

Starter and street culture were now going hand in hand. Public Enemy's Chuck D, a New York native, did photoshoots in a Los Angeles Raiders Starter jacket. Meanwhile, 2 Live Crew repped their home city by posing for an album cover wearing University of Miami Starter jackets. Starter's sales went from $3 million in 1981 to $200 million in 1991. The brand even kept its cool image despite crossing over into the mainstream, the brand appearing in Hollywood films such as *Big, Beverly Hills Cop II, My Cousin Vinny* and most famously *Coming To America*, in which Eddie Murphy and Arsenio Hall's characters wear them to fit in on the streets of New York.

Anything that becomes a phenomenon on the streets of the US will find an audience in the UK. Specialist US sports retailers and importers across the UK couldn't get the jackets in fast enough. These iconic pieces of sports merchandise became travelling ads for the NFL at a time when the league was in danger of being forgotten on British shores.

However, back in the US, demand for Starter had taken a dangerous turn in some cities. A Chicago police sergeant told *Sports Illustrated* in 1990 that his department dealt with 50 incidents a month involving Starter jackets. The *New York Times* said that cities including New York, Chicago and Detroit in 1990 were seeing a steep rise in young people being robbed for Starter jackets, mirroring the other disturbing crime trend of Air Jordan shoe robberies. In the space of a year four people were murdered in Chicago for their Starter gear. 'It was a serious problem,' says Chris. 'Kanye West's mother, in her autobiography, said the reason she didn't let Kanye on the train in Chicago was because she didn't want him to get robbed for a Starter jacket.'

As horrible as these crimes were, it also proved how incredibly desirable these items were. 'Starter was at the centre of so many zeitgeist moments from the 1980s and 1990s,' says Chris. 'Pop culture went hand in hand with Starter jackets for people in the US and a certain section of people in the UK. You can't think of fashion from that era without thinking of Starter.' In an episode of hit Apple TV+ comedy *Ted Lasso*, the titular coach bemoans the loss of a Chicago Bulls Starter jacket he let a girl borrow back when he was in high school. Soon afterwards, Kola Bokinni, who plays AFC Richmond captain Isaac in the show, and 'team-mate' Billy Harris, who plays the club's Welsh star Colin, turned up at NVL. Kola ended up with a Bulls Starter jacket of course, while Harris opted for a Chicago Bears version. In 2022 the cast had a luxury box at Tottenham Hotspur Stadium for an International Series game – decked out in NVL items. Cristo Fernandéz, who plays Dani Rojas on the show, did a sideline interview wearing a classic Detroit Lions jacket during the game on NFL Network during which NVL was namechecked for a global audience.

The NFL as a sport wasn't fashionable in the UK in the 1990s but enough of its clothes were. No team benefited from this more in the UK than the Raiders did. 'Al Davis has to be given a lot of credit for utilising the Raiders as a brand rather than just as a professional sports team,' says Chris. 'He created the idea of being a Raider and made that cool. That's why the rappers were wearing their logo. It's why NWA wore so much Raiders gear – because the Raiders were bad boys. Davis made that branding culturally relevant. In the same way Michael Jordan turned the Chicago Bulls into a brand. The difference was that Jordan was responsible because he was the star player at that time. Meanwhile, people – and especially British people – were not thinking: "the Raiders are great because Bo Jackson plays for them". People could see that Raiders logo, without even associating it with any Raiders players or bits of history. They just know the brand. Davis was a pioneer.'

Even while Starter was a hot brand in the UK, the problems had already started in the US, thanks to issues the average British sports fan was unaware of. 'Starter always prided itself on being authentic, which meant the fans could buy what the teams were wearing at that time,' says Chris. 'So when the Major League Baseball strike started in 1994 [a nearly eight-month stoppage that caused the cancellation of the 1994 World Series] it had a hugely negative effect on sales and profits. On top of that, the robberies and murders made people wary. They then had gangs of thieves targeting trucks delivering merchandise.' Other events seemed to suggest that even Mother Nature was against them. At various times, Starter had to deal with a fire destroying most of the products in its New Haven, Connecticut factory. Next a tornado destroyed its Hamden, Connecticut, factory. A hurricane ruined the factory it had opened in Jamaica. There was even a huge shipment that arrived from the Philippines infested with lice.

In 1992 Nike was rebuffed when it tried to buy Starter. By the end of the decade Starter declared bankruptcy. In 2004 Nike finally managed to buy the brand – only to sell it on again just three years later while it was moving on its unwanted soccer brand Umbro to Iconix. Nowadays Starter once again has licences for the biggest sports leagues but, crucially, you won't see these items on the sidelines. Their authenticity – and thus appeal on the streets of the US and the UK – is dramatically reduced. It's not the only problem Chris has with the current incarnation of Starter, and he even got into a social media spat with former New York Giants linebacker Carl Banks, who now runs Starter.

'I have an issue with the fact that they are using virgin plastics and creating fast fashion items that will eventually end up in landfill,' says Chris. 'These new Starter jackets are not the real deal. Let's put it this way: the old-style Starter jackets are like Lawrence Taylor, while the new-style ones are like Carl Banks. There was a moment in time when big brands could have taken a stand by not creating new things with high carbon footprint production. I tweeted something about this regarding Starter and assumed Banks would never see it. But he did and he responded. He got quite angry with NVL and basically said that we were hypocrites because we were still selling old Starter stuff. Which is missing the point.'

Chris is keen to protect a particular era's style and the public has responded. He doesn't feel retro-styled products, such as the ones Starter is creating, will prove anywhere near as popular. 'The bottom line is, Carl, no offence, but I don't want your style of Starter jackets,' he says. 'And anyone who has any understanding of the brand, or the history of sideline wear, doesn't want a new Starter jacket either. People in the UK and America want the old-style jackets because of the nostalgia factor. There are plenty of people wearing Starter jackets who were not into American football when the brand was big, but like me they probably got into the sport thanks to someone else. For some people they'll associate the jacket with a time when that person was a fan. So they might think it reminds them of going to a game with their dad or watching on TV with their uncle. It's like the famous saying: "the only thing that's more powerful than new is nostalgia".'

Chris wouldn't be where he is today if he hadn't discovered a particular NFL UK community. He's now paying it forward thanks to the way that NVL has become more than just a retailer. The big break came in 2020 when the world was figuring out how they were going to stay entertained during the early days of the pandemic. 'When Hugh and I were locked down in a bubble together we were doing a YouTube show called *The Emergency Broadcast*, which came out every Thursday night,' says Chris. 'It was just a stupid magazine show, the sort of thing NFL UK would never produce. We started off looking very low-budget and crappy, but eventually got quite good. From there we started booking guests and they were good ones, too. It turned into a podcast, ran for a season and was very successful. The last person on the podcast was [former Chicago Bears Pro Bowl defensive tackle] Tommie Harris, and his story was a good ending for the show. During the time we were making *The Emergency Broadcast*, we got an email from a TV production company asking if they could come and do a feature on the shop. While they were here they said they were working on Channel 5's *NFL End Zone* highlights show and asked if we could film a segment for them about the next *Thursday Night Football* game. We had to do two versions: one for in case the Jets won and one for in case they lost. It clearly proved popular because we were asked to do the whole of the 2020 season. It ended up being a really wonderful way to spend a Wednesday because Channel 5 would come down, bring a producer and camera crew, and film it there at our warehouse with all the memorabilia behind us. The look was like a cross between Philip Schofield's CBBC broom cupboard and an NFL bedroom.'

The naturally lo-fi, retro-inspired aesthetic of these TV segments was unintentionally reminiscent of the early days of Channel 4's coverage of the sport. It opened doors for Chris that he is very appreciative of. 'To be offered airtime on *NFL End Zone* was very humbling,' he says. 'The bottom line is, for me as a fan, it gets me the access that I never would have dreamed of. We went from doing NVL pop-ups at Wembley to going to the London games with a press pass. I could never have expected any of this. The YouTube show was just for the fans of the shop. It just happened to be that we did it when a lot of people were at home on furlough, most people had more time and many had more cash because they weren't going out to spend money. Instead they were sitting on their phones bored and trying to feel better. Which meant people started buying stuff from us. The business started growing and that led to more followers on social media. We heard that from a lot of people telling us that it got them through lockdown. A tight community has sprung up around NVL which is really heartening. One of the exciting things we did was create a fantasy football league with lots of the guests that we had on the show. It meant we could play with stars such as Maurice Jones-Drew.'

The NFL cottoned on to the grassroots appeal NVL has naturally cultivated. Now when the league sends teams to London for games, they're also sent to NVL's warehouse to check out the vintage clothing for the team and wear it in a photoshoot. UK fans in the 1980s and 1990s sought out American style to supplement their own local fan culture and NVL is now sharing that with the stars of the modern league.

Chris has helped fans in the present connect with the past, whether that's paying homage to a legendary player or giving a nod to an older relative's favourite star because that family member got them hooked on the game. He's also allowed long-time fans to relive memorable moments from the 1980s and 1990s. 'It's all well and good trying to grow the game and get new fans,' says Chris, 'but we need to pay respect to the fans who have been here from the beginning. The older fans are the ones that this entire community is built on. Whether it's back in the '80s with the people going to the first games at Wembley, or those who were holding it down during the '90s when the sport lost its mass appeal, or the people who decided to connect people with podcasts and meet-ups. It's not just about the next new fan, it's about all the fans that have come before.'

The power of fan clubs

ALTHOUGH BORN in London, Darren Conway grew up in west Belfast, with his formative years spent on the Glencairn estate, at the top of Shankill Road. The area was known as a Loyalist stronghold, notorious for sectarian violence. In his Protestant neighbourhood, Catholics were considered the enemy. Darren wasn't Catholic but he still stuck out like a sore thumb. He says he felt like the only black kid in Northern Ireland.

In a place and time when being different to those around you had the potential to put you in lethal danger, standing out wasn't a comfortable position to be in. 'I kind of scratched my way to, not the top but near the top,' Darren says of the pecking order of his school in Belfast. 'In my year, I was not to be trifled with.' That meant that when finally another person of colour joined the school, Darren felt obligated to keep an eye on the boy to make sure he was safe.

The course of Darren's life changed during a biology lesson. 'Mrs Fry said to put your hand up if you've ever been on holiday outside of the UK,' says Darren, 'and I think I was one of two or three kids whose hand didn't go up. Which led to a reward for being honest, I guess.' Darren forgot all about the question until he was called into a school office a few weeks later and asked if he would like to go on a trip with the Irish Children's Fund – six weeks in the USA. There was a catch however. He would have to stay with a Catholic family. Darren had been an outsider his whole life. The idea of being an outsider far away from the Troubles, far away from Belfast, far away from school? No problem. 'Although I lived in a Loyalist enclave, the whole sectarianism thing didn't make sense to me,' Darren admits. 'Everyone was picking on me for being black in the street or in school so I had my own battles to fight.'

In the run up to the trip, which was due to take place during the summer of 1984, Darren – and other kids chosen by the charity to experience a different culture – sent and received letters to and from a host family. No one was really sure what to expect. All Darren knew was the family lived in Oak Park, Illinois – right next to Chicago. He soon realised his knowledge of the USA was already a step above others who went on the trip. The kids' long journey started with a 250-mile bus ride from Belfast to Shannon Airport, across the border in the Republic of Ireland. Once they were up in the air Darren was soon losing patience with his fellow passengers. When he heard them talking about going to 'Illa-noise' he couldn't hold his tongue and got into a big argument about their faulty pronunciation.

Although he admits he's not quite sure how he knew the correct way to say Illinois, it's also fair to say that Darren was an incredibly intelligent child. He had been offered places at the very best schools in Northern Ireland, such as Belfast Royal Academy and the Royal Belfast Academical Institution. He turned them down flat. 'What happens when you live in a single parent household?' he asks rhetorically. 'We haven't got any guidance. Where are the decision makers?' He decided that the risks of being an even bigger target on his estate due to a posh school blazer outweighed the benefits of an improved education.

Oak Park was like a different world. A spacious, affluent village famous for its Frank Lloyd Wright architecture and for being the birthplace of Ernest Hemingway. It was here that Darren had his eyes opened to that greatest of American sports: baseball.

Wait, what? The host family were ardent Chicago White Sox fans and during that balmy six weeks, Darren was regularly taken to baseball games at the old Comiskey Park on Chicago's South Side. With the summer baseball season in full flow when he arrived, Darren's main connection with the Chicago Bears was through Mikey, a boy in the host family who was the same age as him. Mikey was a huge Walter Payton fan and an avid collector of Topps NFL trading cards. He would show them to Darren and talk about all the players, but was more animated when talking about Payton. However, Darren couldn't accept that any sportsman could be better than his beloved Bryan Robson, captain of Manchester United and England. 'How on Earth can Payton be better than the England captain? The man who had scored the fastest goal in the 1982 World Cup?' Darren asked Mikey in astonishment. When Darren was told how many times Payton had run for 100 yards in a game he retorted by saying that Robson runs at least 300 yards in every match.

'I didn't quite get American football,' Darren admits, 'because it wasn't in season.' But preseason soon rolled around and Darren got his first taste of the NFL, albeit via televised exhibition games. Mikey's dad had grown up a Cardinals fan rather than a Bears fan. In his youth the Cardinals were the Chicago Cardinals, playing most of their games at Comiskey Park. He felt strongly that the city was big enough to have two NFL teams like it had two pro baseball teams. However, with the Cardinals at this point in St Louis, the family patriarch threw his weight behind the Bears. Darren had got a glimpse of something that would dominate his life for decades.

It wasn't just about sport. Darren saw a lot of what Chicago had to offer and fell in love with the place. He was taken to the symphony, a big 4th of July fireworks show at Grant Park, fishing trips and days at the beach. Along with other kids from the charity he went away to a camp for a few days, although having seen a fair few American slasher movies he spent that time worried he would be murdered by a masked maniac.

The trip wasn't an unqualified success, however. Some members of the extended family had no idea what life was like in Northern Ireland, at one point explaining to him what a carrot was and asking if he had them back home, which made Darren seethe. What was worse was that one of Mikey's older brothers ('a Hollywood-style American high school jerk') seemed determined to cause problems for Darren throughout his stay. It started with him hiding Darren's swimming pass, preventing him from returning to the local pool on the hot afternoons. It culminated in a cruel prank on Darren's birthday, which fell during the trip. 'I woke up that morning looking forward to my birthday,' Darren says. 'I was super smart but also super sensitive. I might be going to take his behaviour on any other day, but I'm not going to take it on my birthday.'

Darren decided to settle it Belfast-style. 'I grabbed him, pulled him out of the house and down the stairs of the porch,' Darren reveals, 'and beat the hell out of him in the street in front of the neighbours. A trick I learned off my mum when she was beating me was that she would let out a swear word with every blow. So I did the same. That led to an awkward couple of weeks. From that point on I was just waiting to go home. I had a really good time and then that happened on my 13th birthday. It just went sour.'

Back home in Belfast Darren finally had the chance to watch regular-season NFL games. The 1984 season was a good one for the Bears, who won the NFC Central and reached the NFC Championship game. The 1985 Bears have gone down in history as arguably the best team in NFL history and Darren was along for the ride, thanking his lucky stars that the trip had taken him to the home of the NFL's most exciting and well-loved franchise. Along with his brother he stayed up to watch Super Bowl XX but failed to stay awake for the whole thing. Thankfully for Darren the Bears' dominant performance meant the final quarter was a coronation rather than a contest. On a post-Super Bowl high, he told everyone who would listen how great Walter Payton was; Bryan Robson had been knocked off top spot in Darren's power rankings. It helped that at this time in history the TV schedules were not packed with soccer, as they would be a decade later.

Darren had seen his team become champions and his interest in the sport went up a notch. Channel 4's NFL coverage was now appointment viewing in the Conway household. He followed the 1986 season intently and even managed to stay awake for the entirety of Super Bowl XXI, a milestone for any school-aged NFL fan in the UK. After that Conway and his family returned to London, where his new friends were also watching the NFL. Super Bowl parties with his new mates became an annual tradition. He was a voracious reader of the local magazines and newspapers – he considered *Touchdown* to be a cut above the rest – but this would soon not be enough.

'In the early 1990s I was working in London and on a Tuesday morning I'd leave at about 7am so I could buy and read *USA Today*,' says Darren. 'I'd pay what seemed like an enormous sum of money just to see the NFL stats. That was your life as an NFL fan back then. You got *First Down* on a Thursday but if you were obsessive and wanted more you would find somewhere that sold *USA Today*.'

As the decade went on Darren became frustrated with coverage of the sport and of the Bears in particular, saying *First Down* may as well have called itself '49ers, Cowboys and Dolphins Weekly'. Around this time UK fans of all franchises were also craving more in-depth – and partisan – coverage of their teams and fanzines started springing up. Darren was not going to let this opportunity pass him by. 'I felt like it was my civic duty to bring more Bears information to the UK fanbase,' he says.

He'd seen fan groups advertise themselves and their newsletters in *First Down* so Darren followed suit. To get the first issue you had to send two first-class stamps to Darren's home. Uptake was good although some people were wary. 'One guy wrote me a letter saying he was quite nervous about getting in touch,' says Darren, 'because he thought it might be a way of scamming first-class stamps. And that he realised if someone was going to scam people out of first-class stamps then probably the last thing they would do is pretend it was for a Chicago Bears fanzine.'

The first issue of *Bearing Up* appeared in 1995 with Rashaan Salaam as its cover star. Heisman Trophy winner Salaam had just been drafted by the Bears and Darren's fanzine celebrated what he hoped would be the start of a new era of success. £12 would get you a year's supply of issues, discounted to £6 if you were a student.

It's a good job Darren didn't get into this to make money. 'One of the subscribers was a Welsh guy in university down in Bournemouth and I always liked to speak to other fans,' Darren says. 'I called him on my old-school brick mobile phone. His housemates nicknamed him The Colonel because he worked part-time at KFC. We were talking for ages. When I got my phone bill I saw that the call had cost me £9. To check on someone who had paid £6.' Darren estimates that his losses over the years running *Bearing Up* reached well into four figures. The man they called the Colonel now runs his own marketing company in Canada and has been a constant in Darren's life ever since. Just one of many lifelong connections Darren made in the early days of *Bearing Up*.

More fan clubs were springing up and all the organisers were happy to give advice to newcomers looking to start up their own. Darren was in fact instrumental in helping the Packers club get set up and became good friends with their organiser for a few years. It just goes to show how important those rivalries are. Many of the fan club heads would meet up at the Lord Moon of the Mall pub, now called The Horse & Guardsman, just a hundred yards (appropriate for a Walter Payton fan) from Darren's office in central London. This was also the main meeting point of an irreverent fanzine called *Extra Point* that covered the entire league. Darren made good use of his working location by spending time on Charing Cross Road, a street famed for its bookshops. There he discovered Sportspages and arranged a deal with them to sell copies of *Bearing Up* alongside fanzines from top soccer clubs. Sportspages, which was open from 1985 to 2006, was the UK's leading retailer for sports books and magazines. It was the only place UK fans could reliably track down *Sports Illustrated* every week and also prided itself on its massive selection of soccer fanzines. It was the place to be.

To put each issue together Darren would pore over any coverage he found about the Bears, once again relying heavily on the international edition of *USA Today*. Although the web hadn't yet gone mainstream he was able to connect with other fans and read more coverage via newsgroups. In a desire to be as up-to-date as possible and give his audience something they didn't know, he would frequently call the Bears HQ just before he was finishing an issue to get a last-minute news story. 'I'd get put through to an office secretary and ask: "Been any transactions, any news?" I just wanted anything,' says Darren.

Other fans pitched in, penning guest articles or pulling together stats. Although *Bearing Up* was Darren's creation, he welcomed all the help he could get. He'd spend hours every day finding pictures and putting everything together using Microsoft Word on a work laptop he would take home. Darren would source every game on VHS tape – at great expense – so he could write his own reports.

The first season of *Bearing Up* was a success because it brought Bears fans together and gave them information they previously didn't have access to. On the field it was a different story. 'They drafted a Heisman Trophy running back,' says Darren. 'You just think: "Bingo! Playoffs! Things are only going to get better!" Then they failed to make the playoffs that year. The Bears played on Christmas Eve against the Eagles on Sky Sports. They won, thinking that would get them in the playoffs but another result blocked their path. I remember sitting watching it with my mum and my sister and being quite angry because Alonzo Spellman had three sacks in that game and I didn't want the Bears to re-sign him. He held out and was just a bit useless. But he had those three sacks and of course got a big contract. Then I think things started to unravel for the Bears in 1996.'

Bearing Up had Darren moving in different circles now, but it didn't change how he carried himself. 'I got a press pass for the London Monarchs from [Sky Sports NFL and NFL Europe host] Nick Halling and [*First Down* editor] Keith Webster,' Darren says. 'The Monarchs were playing the Amsterdam Admirals at the old White Hart Lane stadium in Tottenham and I sat in the press box eating hot dogs because apparently you get those in the press box. I'd be disappointed if I ever get to go in a press box again and there are no hot dogs. After the game ended I went down to the Admirals locker room because I wanted to talk to players the Bears had assigned to them.'

While most of the journalists in the locker rooms were middle-aged and white, Darren was in his 20s and black – just like the majority of the players there. So it was only natural that many of the Admirals players felt a certain kinship with Darren. 'One of them told me they were going out in central London once they left the stadium and that I should come with them,' he says. 'We ended up going to TGI Fridays and some of the Monarchs players joined us. We were just talking about football and life. They were all genuinely interested in me. Like, "What's this guy all about?" At one point I was speaking to a lineman allocated by the Detroit Lions. We shook hands and he told me how much it hurt to do that. Not because I'm a tough guy with an iron grip but because he knew that after every game he would be in an incredible amount of pain. But there was another player peering at me the whole time. It seemed like he was jealous I was getting all this attention and I'm not even a player.'

Darren's day job required him to dress smartly and a trip to the press box felt like another occasion that he should dress up for. He already had the potential to feel self-conscious sitting around established NFL journalists so the least he could do was to make sure he didn't look like a fan who had wandered through the wrong door at White Hart Lane. So Darren was at the game and the evening out in a three-piece suit so that he could look, in his own words, 'respectful and respectable' among the media. This didn't go down well with one player. 'Eventually the guy from the Admirals who had been peering at me over dinner stood up, gestured at my clothes and said: "Man, you're nothing but a house nigger."

I was absolutely outraged,' says Darren. 'I squared up to him and started poking him in the chest asking: "What did you say to me?" I grew up in Northern Ireland hearing the N word every day from bullies. I'm not going to put up with that. He knew nothing about me.'

Cooler heads ensured the situation didn't escalate but Darren was still furious. He'd endured similar comments from ignorant people in his youth and didn't expect it from a black man his own age. Especially when he'd worked hard to be in a position to spend time around them as a peer. Also at TGI Fridays were some of the Monarchs cheerleaders celebrating a birthday. They came over to Darren and the players to invite them along to legendary Covent Garden nightclub Stringfellows, where the festivities would continue. Darren led the way and ushered the players on to a double-decker bus. 'The driver dropped us off on Shaftesbury Avenue,' says Darren, 'and the players were all asking: "What's going on? Where are we going?" I just said: "Don't worry, follow me." We walked about 100 yards and an offensive lineman for the Admirals just stopped and asked where the club was. I said it was close. He shook his head at me and said: "Man, shit, you don't know where you going, you ain't got no clue." Again, I just lost the plot. I squared up to this 6ft 6in, 300lb player. I told him: "Listen, you're in London now, this is my fucking town. Just fucking get behind me. You're the fucking foreigner here." And he just shut up. We had a fantastic night at Stringfellows in the end. Everyone had a great time and I didn't get home until 5am.'

Big news hit in 1997. The Bears would be playing an exhibition game in Dublin's Croke Park that summer. For Darren it meant a first trip across the Irish Sea since moving back to London ten years previously. It would also be an opportunity to meet *Bearing Up* readers, recruit more subscribers and speak to players in person. To keep costs down Darren stayed in a hostel with a fellow Bears fan. When the time came to pick up his press pass from the NFL's assigned hotel his friend swiped a pass meant for someone on *The Sun* newspaper so he could join Darren at events.

When Darren arrived at the Bears' practice session, it was the first time he had been face to face with his heroes. 'I had a chat with Rashaan Salaam and he was more interested in asking me questions about where was good to hang out in Dublin,' says Darren. 'Then the next day, he recognised me and came over to talk again. Obviously things like that made my week.' Some interactions were more revealing and gave Darren an insight into the fragile confidence of the larger-than-life players he had been watching on TV. 'I saw quarterback Rick Mirer and said: "Good luck for week one." And he just looked at me as if to say: "I'm not starting week one." I thought: "We just traded the 11th pick in the draft for you and you do not believe in yourself." He had the look of a frightened kid.'

Darren also mixed with members of the American media at practice, some of whom were quite condescending and seemed sceptical that a British fan would know much about the sport let alone the nitty-gritty of the depth chart. 'Once I started talking they quickly realised I knew more about their sport than they did,' Darren says.

After years of toiling away trying to give Bears fans in the UK the stories they wanted to read, Darren himself became a story. Melissa Isaacson, then of the *Chicago Tribune*, caught wind of a British fan who Bears players were gravitating towards and asked to interview him. She worked on the story for two days and was protective of it. 'I remember a journalist from the AP [Associated Press] came sniffing around,' says Darren, 'and she basically told him: "He's mine, he's my story."' When the story was published in America in the run-up to the game it meant that Bears fans in Chicago knew more about Darren than most of the *Bearing Up* subscribers. Although by now he had certainly become quite the celebrity with Bears fans who had travelled over to Ireland. As he would write in the next issue of *Bearing Up*, quoting Homer Simpson: 'I always wondered if there was a God, and now I know. There is, and it's me.'

Darren had handed out hundreds of *Bearing Up* fliers in Dublin and it led to, in his words, 'a tidal wave of new subscribers'. It kicked off a golden era in Darren's eyes, a four-year run of *Bearing Up* being an essential read for fans of the team and Darren himself being an approachable figurehead of Bears fandom in the UK. 'In the *Bearing Up* days I would speak to other fans endlessly,' says Darren. 'I remember having a big row at work with my boss because I was on the phone so much. It wouldn't just be the readers either. If their dad or girlfriend or whoever answered I'd be talking to them as well. It could be about anything – world affairs even.' It took a Herculean effort for Darren to get the fanzine out each time. 'I had to stop getting it printed at work,' he says. 'I would commute into central London from Essex, then go down to a print place in south London to drop off the issue on a floppy disk. That night I'd have to sort hundreds of stamped addressed envelopes. Then the next morning, I'd have the same journey to pick up all the printed copies, put them all in their envelopes and get them in a postbox. Then I'd get back on a train to go to work. And this is just the time when I wasn't writing and editing the fanzine.' To make matters worse Darren was having to work seven days a week across two jobs to make ends meet.

Eventually Darren got to the end of the road with *Bearing Up* in 2001. 'I realised I didn't have enough time to produce a really good fanzine any more,' he says. 'I was creating a lot less original content. The only properly original things I had were my game reports. I wasn't getting the sense of enjoyment out of it that I previously did. And by this time the internet was so big everyone in the UK could read everything from Chicago anyway.'

A member of the club helped Darren put *Bearing Up* online and encouraged members of the community to join the forum hosted there under the name Bear Down UK. By this time Darren had become disillusioned with the whole enterprise. One of his goals in the *Bearing Up* days was to be recognised as an official chapter of the main Chicago Bears fan club. He would speak to the Bears on a regular basis about this and each time he'd be told he'd be added if he could hit a certain target for subscriber numbers. But each time he did, the Bears wanted yet more. Then one day Darren got word that they had given official chapter status to a fan in Scotland who Darren had never heard of – someone who wasn't even enough of a Bears fan to be part of the *Bearing Up* community. Darren called him and asked: 'Who are you and what have you got to offer UK fans?' His response was: 'Nothing, I'm just doing it to get free stuff.' Darren felt betrayed and it was a slap in the face for someone who had done more for Bears fans in the UK than the team itself had done. Many years later the Bears would rectify this mistake and use the Bear Down UK admin team as their official point of contact for reaching out to their British fans and in 2021 the franchise became one of just six to be granted marketing access to the UK by the NFL. In 2022 the team hosted its first ever official watch party in the UK and have plans to hold more across the country.

As online communication rapidly replaced the more personal touch that Darren was famous for, the original figurehead for Bears fans was happy to take a step back and just be an avid fan again. 'I was quite active on Twitter for a while and was talking to some of the guys who became "Bears Twitter famous," says Darren. 'I also have a secondary account that I set up but abandoned because everything on social media is so toxic. Certain things became politicised and I didn't want any part of it, I didn't want to be involved in the debate. Now I've got a separate Twitter account that I use to search for Bears news but that's pretty much it.'

Like anyone who started a UK fan club for an NFL team, Darren made a huge commitment to his members. For many people in a fan club, especially before the internet was mainstream, the only time you might speak to a fellow fan of the same team was via the club's founder. For those who take it upon themselves to devote time and money to running a fan club, the job is never really done and they always wish they could've done even more. 'I wish I had the foresight to keep all my correspondence, all the letters from people in the club,' says Darren. 'There was a guy called Brian Montague who was a big supporter of the fan club. I was struggling financially with keeping the club going and he sent me about £100. It helped me put out an extra batch of issues. One time he said we should meet up to go for a few drinks and dinner. I was unsophisticated and immature at the time so thought that was a weird thing to do – a man in his twenties to go out for a meal with a middle-aged guy he's never even met. So I just never committed to anything.

'Eventually I met him but only for about five minutes. It was outside my flat and he had come to drop some stuff off, some things like old NFL rulebooks, which I've still got. And then he died. I had no idea he'd been ill. It really affected me because it made me think about how immature I was. Now, because I'm older, going out for that meal would be totally normal but back then it seemed like an odd thing to do so I just didn't do it. His mum wrote to me to tell me he had died, said he'd been suffering from an illness, what a good son he'd been, that he was buried with some of his Bears stuff and left money to an animal charity. This has haunted me for years and I think about it a lot. He was obviously just reaching out to someone who shared his passion for the game and his team and I was too immature to accept it. He didn't want people to know he was helping *Bearing Up* financially; he just felt bad that I was putting in so much time and money, so for his sake I didn't mention it in any of the issues. I've never told anyone about it until now. The Bears meant so much to him and I could've done more.'

The Claymores slice through Europe

IAN SUTHERLAND has been watching the NFL regularly as long as any fan in the UK but it was in the mid-1990s that his relationship with the game changed dramatically.

'The first time I saw American football was actually in the mid-70s,' says Ian, 'when *World of Sport* was on every Saturday on ITV. In their international slot I saw highlights of a Super Bowl. It was only about 15 minutes but it intrigued me. At that point, it just looked like a lot of people running around hitting each other. I didn't really understand much about it.'

All that changed in 1982 when Channel 4 brought the sport to the masses on a weekly basis and Ian was ready for it. 'I spent the first season trying to understand the game and figuring out if there was a team that I felt close to,' he says. 'For most people in the UK there's very rarely any genuine connection with the team. You just develop a connection as you watch. The NFC Championship game was Washington hosting Dallas at the old RFK Stadium. I remember watching it on TV and just before the teams came out, the home fans were jumping up and down, making the stadium shake, and chanting "Bring on the Cowboys". When the teams took the field, Washington physically dominated the game with the Hogs and John Riggins. I thought: "Yeah, that's it."'

The atmosphere at RFK had hooked Ian for life. He finally got to see the Redskins in the flesh when they faced the San Francisco 49ers at Wembley in the 1992 American

Bowl, while his favourite team were the reigning Super Bowl champions. Then in 1996 he made the pilgrimage to RFK in the old stadium's final season, attending the penultimate NFL game ever held there. 'It was a crazy, spontaneous decision to go,' admits Ian. 'I was in DC for 36 hours. I just had to go to the game. It was fantastic to be there. I was in an old wooden stand with no video screens, entertainment or speakers – just the marching band. It was against the 49ers again and there was a point where it looked like we had recovered a fumble at a key moment and the place was just going apeshit. Unfortunately we didn't get the ball and Steve Young took the game to overtime, and the 49ers then won it. I remember Steve Young being very emotional afterwards, saying how great it was to play in that stadium in that atmosphere.'

When fans get to attend games in person their connection to a team grows stronger. This wasn't just evident in the NFL at the time, it was also true for the World League of American Football and NFL Europe. Not that Ian felt much of a connection to the London Monarchs in the WLAF's first incarnation. 'I followed it mostly in the pages of *First Down*,' says Ian. 'I felt slightly conflicted, because I thought I should support the Monarchs but as a Scotsman, I just felt a bit weird. I've got nothing against England or English people, it's just not where my heart lies. I eventually went down to Wembley in the second season to see them play the New York-New Jersey Knights.'

Although Ian felt a bit uncomfortable supporting an English team, it wasn't because he felt there should be a team in Scotland. He says the idea didn't even cross his mind at any point. When the WLAF closed its doors after the 1992 season, Ian, like many UK fans, forgot about the league and carried on watching the NFL on Channel 4. Ian, like some others, got his live fix by attending games in the British leagues.

Everything changed for Ian, and many others north of the border, when he read in *First Down* that not only was the WLAF returning but there would be a team called the Scottish Claymores based at Murrayfield Stadium in Edinburgh. 'I was stunned,' says Ian. 'Absolutely stunned but also gratefully stunned. I couldn't believe our luck. I didn't understand exactly why they had chosen Scotland but I loved that they were doing it.'

Ian, although thrilled, had some minor reservations about the whole enterprise. 'One of the problems with the league was that you could never say what it was,' admits Ian. 'Did it exist to grow the NFL brand? Was it a spring league to develop players for the NFL? Or was it something that had to make money? I don't think the organisers ever made up their minds. What concerned me when they announced the creation of the Claymores was the publicity stuff they put out saying they expected crowds would be between 20,000 and 30,000. I thought: "Do they know how many people go to watch professional sport in Scotland?" It was unrealistic. The average was about 10,000 at the peak. But even that was better than probably all but six Scottish sports teams: the national soccer and rugby teams plus [soccer clubs] Celtic, Rangers and probably Heart of Midlothian and Hibernian. Maybe Aberdeen would beat those crowds sometimes.'

None of this was going to stop Ian from grabbing the opportunity with both hands. No matter how many people he thought would be in the Murrayfield seats, he knew he would be a constant there. 'At the time, I was living in Edinburgh,' says Ian, 'so I bought a season ticket as soon as they were available, and so did my friends. I don't remember much about the team coming together at this time. It was always a murky process. It felt like there was some agreement with NFL coaches as to which players and coaches would be working together. As far as I could tell, the NFL teams allocating players were more concerned with who their players were working with. They didn't care how successful the WLAF teams were, they just wanted their guy to improve.'

The first year for the Claymores was a disaster in some respects and a success in others. The record and performances were poor but a dedicated hardcore group of fans had formed over the course of the two-win season. 'That 2-8 record is burned into my memory but we loved it,' says Ian. 'When I got my season ticket, I still wasn't sure how I was going to feel about it all. Then during the first game against the Rhein Fire they became my team. My heart got into it. We had a terrible year on the field but I was there for all the home games and then went down to London for the final game of the season against the Monarchs.'

Although Ian didn't have any fear that the plug would be pulled on his Claymores after just one season, he also had no idea what to expect from the second year. 'We didn't know what the Claymores or the other teams would be like,' he says. 'You might see the odd bigger name on a roster, perhaps someone you've heard of if you've followed college football but you couldn't tell who was going to affect a team. We turned up to the first game of year two to see what we had – we had no idea if they'd be better or worse than the previous year.'

The team would be much better than they had been in 1995 and this was emphasised when they faced the Frankfurt Galaxy, the reigning World Bowl champions, on the road in the Waldstadion. 'This is still one of my favourite days of my whole life,' says Ian. 'One of the big things about the league was that all fans are friends and everybody gets on. In 1995, the Claymores asked a small group of fans, me included, to look after the travelling Galaxy fans when they came to Murrayfield that year. We ended up making a few friends that day so we got invited over to the away game in Frankfurt so they could repay the favour. We went to the game on a Galaxy supporters' club bus. We got to tailgate in the forest [Waldstadion translates to Forest Stadium in English] which led to us drinking for seven hours before the game even started.'

The Claymores had started the season in spectacular fashion, taking a 3-1 record into the game in Frankfurt. The team had won more games in a month than they had all of the previous season. Even better, a win over the 4-0 Galaxy would give the Claymores the top-ranked record at the halfway point – and with it an automatic spot in the World Bowl at home. Unbeaten Frankfurt were the highest-scoring team in the league and enjoyed the best home advantage in the WLAF. The crowd for the game would be the highest of the season so far but not because of visiting fans. 'Frankfurt had been scoring for fun,' says Ian, 'but we had been looking good too. However, from speaking to the people in the Claymores ticket office, there were no more than 15 Claymores fans in the stadium that day. But we beat them 20-0. They couldn't even score a point against us. It was just a brilliant day and that's when I said to myself: "Right, now we have a team."'

The Claymores and their fans were then faced with the fact that the final five games of the regular season were in effect meaningless. Although they were 4-1 they could now finish 4-6 and still take their place in the World Bowl. The Claymores didn't let up too much though and went into the championship game with a league-leading 7-3 mark. Inevitably it was the Frankfurt Galaxy (who played in eight of the 14 World Bowls that took place after the competition returned in 1995) as the opposition. 'My memory of the second half of the season isn't so clear,' says Ian, 'but the Claymores' defense certainly seemed to fall off a cliff compared with the first half of the year. When it came to the World Bowl they just couldn't stop Frankfurt's offense. Although they couldn't stop ours either.'

In the final minute of a back-and-forth game, the Galaxy, trailing 32-27, thought they had converted a fourth down only to have it called back because they had illegally advanced a fumble. The Claymores were able to see out the clock and take the title. 'It was a weird ending,' says Ian, 'and a slightly sad way to end the game. But it was obviously a fantastic day. We ended up at a party with team members and cheerleaders present to celebrate.'

Other than the final score, another number Claymores fans were focused on was the attendance, officially listed as 38,892 – the biggest crowd ever for an American football game in Scotland and the biggest for a World League game in the UK since the inaugural World Bowl in 1991. The bumper crowd was a pleasant surprise for Ian. 'My initial doubts about what size crowds the team could get in Scotland almost went away at that point,' he says, 'because the World Bowl attendance suggested that maybe their initial ambitions weren't so outlandish. I was hoping to be proved wrong, but I wasn't.'

Hopes were high among Ian and his fellow Claymores die-hards that the championship would be the start of something huge for the sport in Scotland but it wasn't to be. The first home game as defending champions saw a crowd of less than 15,000 at Murrayfield for a game against the Barcelona Dragons and within a few weeks it was barely more than 9,000 when they hosted the Amsterdam Admirals. 'The crowds were anticlimactic,' says Ian, 'coming off the back of the big World Bowl crowd. We were hoping to see a change and it just didn't happen. The gap between the World Bowl [on 23 June 1996] and the first home game of the season [12 April 1997] was too long. Nothing could be done to maintain the interest. But for me and other season ticket holders, we had made a network of friends from other teams. So going on an away game weekend a couple of times each year started to become a common thing. My memories of the Claymores days are as much about the social side as the football side. Getting to watch games featuring your team is obviously fantastic but hanging out with people from other countries and having a good time with them was just as important.'

The crowds weren't huge – and clearly trailed the attendances for the German teams – but the fans who were turning up were making their presence felt. While the Monarchs struggled to get their crowds as invested as they were in the 1991 season, the Claymores realised their small but passionate fanbase was a clear asset. 'Eventually the Claymores decided to put all the fans in the east stand,' says Ian, 'which is the one away from the tunnel. Getting the fans together in that area led to a lot more noise from the stands. We're talking about 8,000 people in a 67,000-capacity stadium. There was a particular game against the Rhein Fire where the away team were driving in a tight game. We generated enough noise between us to lead to a false start. It's not something that will have stuck in everyone's memory but I loved it because it showed what sort of fans we had in the stadium.'

However, it's fair to say that Ian wasn't a typical fan. 'I ended up doing a bit of work with the team,' Ian says. 'It's a bit crazy. I was part of the Fun Bunch. It developed naturally because we went to the games, we danced around in kilts and got everyone in the stands with us to have fun. We ended up working with choreographer Ramona Braganza, who was there to help the cheerleaders, on routines. She said: "We need you guys on the sidelines." This led to us doing all sorts of media stuff. The newspapers would want to take photographs of us quite regularly. We were actually featured on a double page spread in *The Sun* – not that we got paid for it.'

The extra attention that was focused on Ian and his fellow Fun Bunch members didn't change the way they felt about the team. At heart they were still normal fans. 'It wasn't that difficult for people to get more connected with the team,' says Ian. 'If you knew who to speak to, it wasn't hard to show up to the offices or training facility and meet the players. Obviously as the Fun Bunch we got to enjoy some extra opportunities and that was fantastic. But they were still just my team. Those extra responsibilities that we had, eventually it got to where the Claymores were looking to control more of what we did and that wasn't really what we wanted. So it kind of faded away a little bit and that's fine. I just went back to being a fan and that was cool. We had our 15 minutes of fame, but I never lost my connections to the team.'

The years after the World Bowl saw crowds remain relatively small but steady. As the 1990s became the 2000s, the Claymores had a resurgence on the field. 'In the 1990s, it had become very Scottish,' says Ian. 'There was an assumption that, like Scotland's national teams, they wouldn't win all that often. Then in 2000, the Claymores were winning games again. We had a decent running game and things just seemed to click. Unlike the 1996 season, it felt tight and tense. I wasn't as convinced about how good the team was but there was also the change in the league structure.'

By this time the league was called NFL Europe and had abandoned the system that saw the team with the best record halfway through the season automatically hosting the World Bowl. Instead, the top two teams at the end of the year would play for the title at a venue decided well in advance. The Claymores were one of only two teams to post a winning record, their 6-4 mark trailing the Rhein Fire's 7-3. The two teams met for the league title in Frankfurt's Waldstadion, with the German team winning 13-10 thanks to a very late Fire touchdown and a missed field goal from the Claymores' English kicker Rob Hart with eight seconds left on the clock. 'I've never been able to watch any of that game again,' says Ian. 'We managed to get 1,500 Scottish fans to that game, which considering it was such short notice for us all knowing the team was playing in the World Bowl isn't too bad. For a lot of the Claymores fans the trip was simply getting on a bus, driving straight to Frankfurt, watching the game, getting back on the bus, and driving home to Scotland again. I stayed with my friends in the Frankfurt area and went to the game on the Galaxy supporters' bus. Obviously the Galaxy fans did not want the Fire to win so they were all behind the Claymores.'

As well as a change in deciding who played for the championship and the league getting a new name, there were other unfamiliar things for the Claymores to deal with. They had lost their local rival, the Monarchs, after the 1998 season. This meant a trip to England had been replaced by a trip to Berlin, home of the Thunder. Even trips for home games had changed for the Claymores faithful with Glasgow's Hampden Park hosting some games starting in 1998. Before long more games were played in Glasgow than Edinburgh.

'I thought the team lost its heart a bit when the team moved some games from Murrayfield,' says Ian. 'I'm sure there were fans in the west of Scotland who were happy about it. Personally, I felt the atmosphere wasn't the same.

Obviously I still went to all the games. And to be fair, we had some really good games there and the crowds did increase. I accept what the team was trying to achieve by doing it, and you can say it was successful. But I didn't like it.'

Although the cities of Edinburgh and Glasgow, just 50 miles apart, have a natural rivalry, Scotland's most heated rivalry – Celtic vs Rangers or Rangers vs Celtic, depending on your perspective – is a much bigger deal. These two Glasgow soccer clubs dominate sport in Scotland. 'Thankfully it didn't really spill over to Claymores games,' says Ian, 'at least not that I ever saw. Although there was one time we were in a pub in Glasgow, and I was with some Barcelona Dragons fans, because that's who the Claymores were playing that weekend. A very drunk Celtic fan saw the green shirt of a Dragons fan and came to talk to him because of the colour connection. Obviously the Dragons fan was struggling to understand a word being said. Other than that there was very occasionally a bit of banter from people comparing the two cities but it was always good natured and was never an issue. Soccer didn't have much crossover. Most people I knew who became passionate Claymores fans weren't passionate soccer fans.'

The disappearance of the Monarchs was less of an issue for Claymores fans than travelling 50 miles was. The Monarchs had struggled to engage fans in the way that the Claymores had done and the constant changing of home stadiums across England didn't help. 'There were a couple of away games that I went to in London where it was clear the visiting Claymores fans were the only ones making any noise,' says Ian. 'Then when they started trying to move the team around it just got worse. When we played them in the 1998 season, the game was held in Birmingham. I went to the game, looked around the stadium and thought: "Why is the league here?"'

Crowds had been low in London but these plummeted further when they played in Bristol and Birmingham as the England Monarchs. The team had lost its identity in more ways than one, unlike the Claymores. Rumours swirled that the league would cut its losses with the Monarchs and either close the team or merge it with the Claymores. Eventually the Monarchs disappeared and the Claymores lived to fight another day.

'There was a lot of change at the Claymores at the time,' says Ian, 'but it was turnover of office staff. The team was always pretty well run. Because Scotland is a smaller market, the team could get media coverage quite easily. The Claymores would be in the newspapers and on TV; it was much harder for the Monarchs to get that attention.'

Most people following the Claymores assumed the team, and potentially the league itself (outside Germany at least), was living on borrowed time. 'My memory of it is that we just wanted to go to games and enjoy them,' says Ian, 'and there were definitely some good games and performances. The hardcore fans still had their part of the stadium rocking so we had a great time. I didn't really think about the team being closed until what ended up being the last year. The rumours were really starting to fly early in that season and so by the time it came, it was kind of expected.'

After a 2003 season in which Glasgow hosted the World Bowl and the 6-4 Claymores only missed out on a championship game berth by virtue of a tiebreaker, things went downhill fast. The 2004 season ended in a pitiful 2-8 record, the third time the Claymores had won just a pair of games in a year. In October 2003 it was confirmed that the Claymores would be abandoned and replaced by a new German team, the Hamburg Sea Devils. To really anchor the team to a particular time period, the Sea Devils would play in a stadium that was at the time called AOL Stadium. The league now had just one non-German team, the Amsterdam Admirals. As NFL Europe's profile improved in Germany it became almost non-existent everywhere else in the continent. By 2007 the league became NFL Europa (the German word for Europe) but closed down at the end of that season.

'The first I heard about the closure was when I got a text from someone saying that I should go over to the Claymores office in Glasgow – the office had moved from Edinburgh by that point – because they were just giving stuff away,' says Ian. 'It was clear that was happening because the team was closing up. That was definitely before they had made the official announcement.'

Although both UK-based teams ended up closing while the league was still active, the Claymores' rivalry with the Monarchs ended up quite one-sided. They had both won a championship each but the Claymores had lasted longer than the Monarchs, had played more games, won more games, had a better win percentage and had reached more World Bowls. The Monarchs may have been the UK's first team but the Claymores became the most resilient. 'I was devastated but realistic,' says Ian of the closure. 'I thought back to the time when the team started and felt it was unbelievable the league was coming here. It may have been kind of inevitable that the team closed but it was still a big loss. The Claymores had taken a big chunk of my life and played a major part in how I spent my time and enjoyed myself in those years.'

When the Monarchs, and the WLAF along with them, were closed in September 1992, the plan was for a restructure and eventual return. During that gap many Monarchs fans drifted away from the sport at a time when soccer was starting to boom once again. The climate for jilted Claymores fans in 2003 was different. There was no plan in place for the team to come back and it was clear the league was moving on without them. The Claymores had played more than a hundred games over the years and became an established part of the sporting landscape in Scotland. Many of those fans who were new to the sport and became hooked on watching the Claymores play home games were also tuning into NFL games, even if just to see former Claymores stars aim to make it at the highest level. Of course, some felt betrayed and they soured on American football.

The Monarchs' main legacy is showing fans and decision-makers in the US how London could feel like an NFL city, while for the Claymores it was creating a generation of fans in Scotland who felt connected to the sport in a way they could never have imagined. When the Claymores were removed from the league the landscape was in stark contrast to the ones Monarchs fans faced in 1992. By 2003 American football fans could watch every NFL Europe game live on Sky Sports and multiple live games on Sundays and Mondays during the NFL season on both satellite and terrestrial TV. Plus the internet meant fans could find out everything they could want to know about the sport.

Meanwhile, although no one could have confidently predicted it, the NFL would begin playing annual regular season games in the UK just four years after the Claymores closed.

For people like Ian, who already followed the NFL closely, there was no way they would turn their back on the sport. 'I was still an NFL fan,' he says, 'and like many fans I was loyal. I think it's hard for a lot of people in the UK to get their heads around the fact that NFL franchises can move to new places. For a team such as the Raiders, I don't understand how their fans can stay loyal to them when they keep moving. There were lots of Claymores fans that I came to know who were not fans of the NFL before that. The Claymores being dumped did push some of them away from the sport again. Quite a few of them just walked away and never had an interest again after that.'

Ian is a football lifer, though. 'I like pure sport for the sake of it,' he says. 'I still love the sport of American football. I love the science of it. Even after all these years as a fan, I'm still learning more. There's so much to it. After the Claymores' closure I didn't watch NFL Europe on TV, but I did still go to one game every year in Germany. We kept that going until the league folded because I still had very good friends there. It was such a fantastic day out. I got to see my friends and I got to see some live football. I kept an eye on NFL Europe scores but I wasn't paying close attention like I did when my team was involved in the league.'

The fact that the Hamburg Sea Devils had been a direct replacement for the Claymores didn't affect Ian either way. 'I didn't feel anything towards them,' he says. 'I knew the Sea Devils were reasonably successful [they won World Bowl XV, the last game ever played in the league] and that was built on the back of the Claymores. The attitude from fans in Scotland was simply "Good luck". I didn't really pay particular interest and I wasn't invested in them winning or losing.'

Ian doesn't have the Claymores any more but he still has his Washington Commanders. Despite being a fan of the franchise since 1982, even when talking about the players of the past, Ian never refers to those historic teams as Redskins. 'It's a conscious effort,' says Ian. 'It's been a bit difficult supporting the team over the past 20 years. I always knew the name was controversial. I've been to FedEx Field a few times and I met Native Americans who were fans. So I said to myself: "I feel comfortable with the name." When the climate changed, I felt that was fair enough and that the name should

THE AMERICAN FOOTBALL REVOLUTION

go. Unfortunately, this has all coincided with the franchise being run by Dan Snyder, who I think is a dreadful owner. To be honest, I'm at the point now where the team won't get any money from me. As much as I love the sport I won't attend Washington games, I won't pay to watch them online and I won't buy new merchandise until Snyder's gone. I just don't think he deserves my money in any way. I'm also not a massive fan of the International Series games. I've only been to one and that was because Washington was playing there in 2016 and I couldn't stop myself. Because of the cost of travelling down from Scotland to London, I think I'd rather spend an extra £500 going to America and have the true NFL experience. I'd rather see a game in, say, Philadelphia, because I think that'd be more exciting. My ambition is one day to see Washington play a home NFC Championship game in person. That would be the best stadium atmosphere I can imagine.'

Pro football still exists in Europe beyond the NFL's International Series, however. In fact, the Hamburg Sea Devils, unlike the Claymores, still exist. Sort of. A team with that name is currently playing in the European League of Football [ELF], along with the Frankfurt Galaxy, Rhein Fire, Cologne Centurions, Berlin Thunder and Barcelona Dragons. The new teams have no direct connection to the original incarnations (the new league reached an agreement with the NFL over the use of the names) and, unlike the NFL Europe versions, have a focus on European players over NFL hopefuls from the US. Although the league structure is dominated by German teams, the nations of Austria, Hungary, Italy, Poland and Turkey also have a presence in the league despite not featuring in NFL Europe.

Time will tell if the UK is represented at some point, although the league has regularly dropped hints that a

London team is being targeted. 'I think the next live game I see will probably be in the ELF,' says Ian. 'I have friends watching the Galaxy and Fire who have been texting me saying: "You gotta come!"'

Superfans wow the Americans

KEITH SMITH was born in 1963 and Crusader Raider was born in 2003 but both their stories go back to 1941 thanks to a remarkable American. 'During the Second World War, shortly after the attack on Pearl Harbor, my uncle Jack Gunn volunteered to join the war and came to the UK,' says Keith. 'Jack was from El Centro, Southern California, and ended up being based at an airfield called George Washington Field, which today is London Stansted Airport. It was during his time in the UK that he met my aunt, who was from east London and had been in the Women's Land Army. They had a wedding date planned but he missed his own wedding day because he had to land on Omaha Beach and then went on to the Battle of the Bulge. They got married eventually and sailed back to the States on the *Queen Mary*.

'Uncle Jack was amazing. When he was in the Boy Scouts he wanted to go to the 1939 World's Fair in New York but his family couldn't afford for him to go all that way from California. So he got sponsorship and cycled all the way from El Centro to New York [nearly 2,700 miles]. He would stop to sleep behind boards or in Scout huts. He got quite famous for doing it. To this day I run a predictions competition called the Jack Gunn Memorial Trophy. The trophy is in my house at the moment because my wife won it last year.'

Jack loved sport, and football in particular. Keith also fell in love with football, and that was thanks to a 1980 visit to California to see his uncle's family. At that point access to the sport in the UK was pretty much non-existent. When Channel 4 arrived it finally allowed Keith and his siblings to get a regular dose of the game they'd been interested in for a couple of years already.

'My sister is a Chicago Bears fan while my brother is a Green Bay Packers fan,' says Keith. 'We've all got our own teams and we selected them back in the early days of Channel 4. I'm very grateful to Channel 4 because it created an American football boom in this country. It opened up a whole new marketplace. If Channel 4 hadn't come in at that time, a whole generation would have missed out on the sport. Our only other option was to listen on Armed Forces Radio, because that was the only network that provided access to football in those days. There was no Sky Sports on TV, there was no talkSPORT on the radio. You would tune in to hear a game but there would be scratching sounds in the background. The signal would go in and out. The Raiders would be driving and I would lose the signal. You'd have to find out whether your team scored or not later on.'

Seeing the Los Angeles Raiders dominate the Washington Redskins in Super Bowl XVIII in January 1984 helped convince Keith he had made the right choice in picking them as his favourite team. He had to wait until his birthday in 1990 to see them live, when the team played its first overseas game – an American Bowl defeat against the New Orleans Saints at Wembley Stadium. 'It wasn't very nice for that to happen on my birthday,' admits Keith. 'I don't hold a grudge. It's been too many years. I was very disappointed though.'

When Keith loves something he gets very invested and will not do things by half. His passion for music combined with his love of American football when the sport was still a novelty in the UK. 'I used to play in a marching band when I was younger,' he says. 'In fact I am still a musician to this day in a 26-piece big band in east London. But in my younger days we used to play the half-time shows for the Mildenhall Marauders, an American football team based on a US military base in Suffolk. They used to play against other bases across the UK. Our drumline and percussion would make lots of noise every time the Marauders were driving.'

Keith has managed to spend much of his life going to live games. As well as the games he attended in the British leagues, he also saw a relative playing high school football in the US on numerous occasions. But it's the NFL where he has spent most of his time, getting to more than 200 games so far.

'My uncle moved away from El Centro because the air quality was terrible,' says Keith. 'When he and my aunt retired they bought a Silver Bullet trailer and travelled all over the States looking for where they wanted to live. They finally ended up in the Pacific Northwest, near Seattle. They bought a piece of land in the middle of a forest and although Jack was an accountant by trade, he built his own house there. It was literally the house that Jack built. So Seattle is my most visited city for games because my family was there for so many years. I used to go to lots of games at the Kingdome and the current stadium [Lumen Field] when they relocated mainly because the Seahawks were in the AFC West with the Raiders for so many seasons. We could always get tickets for about $10 because the Seahawks wouldn't sell out. The Raiders had a great record at the Kingdome, so often we'd be the only fans left in there at the end. One of my first games at the stadium had a lot of Raiders fans tailgating. They used to do tattoos out there: no cleaning materials, no thought about sanitary conditions, nothing. They would just get your arm and tattoo the score of Raiders victories on it.'

Shortly after Keith's birthday disappointment at Wembley he found himself a regular at the stadium as the World League of American Football arrived. 'I was a season ticket holder for the London Monarchs,' says Keith, 'and was lucky enough to go to road games against the Frankfurt Galaxy, Rhein Fire, Barcelona Dragons and the Amsterdam Admirals. I even went to a Berlin Thunder game after they took our spot in the league. Monarchs home games were fantastic at the beginning although I think Capital Radio probably took more tickets than anybody else to give away for free.'

For many years Keith was just a fan. A dedicated fan who invested a lot of time, money and energy in his beloved Raiders – but still just a fan. 'I started going to Raiders games as soon as they moved back to the Oakland Coliseum after a spell in Los Angeles,' says Keith, 'but for all those years I was in silver and black just like everybody else. I went to the games and I enjoyed the games. Unless I opened my mouth, nobody would have known I was from London, the Bay Area or anywhere else. I just enjoyed football and enjoyed the whole Raider experience. But then in 2003 I decided I was going to take this to another level. I asked my wife Sarah, who is a very good seamstress, if she could create the first Crusader Raider uniform. She did and it made its stadium debut in a victory against the Buffalo Bills in September 2004.'

Keith's idea for the Crusader Raider costume was based on the designs of the Knights Templar. It also featured the red and white St George's cross, the flag of England. Real chainmail was obviously not going to be practical so Sarah had to improvise. 'The first costume had the chainmail made out of individual rubber rings that she painstakingly stitched together to create the chainmail effect over the top of some silver material,' says Keith. 'As soon as the Raiders got their winning score against the Bills, everybody was pulling one another around in the Oakland Coliseum, and that thing got ripped to pieces. It didn't even last the first game. Obviously the chainmail would need to be different. It must've looked a bit like a *Where's Wally?* book. There was a sea of silver and black, and maybe a handful of Buffalo Bills fans because they didn't travel too well to the Bay Area. And there was me: the only Raiders fan in red and white. People used to shout at me in a very polite Oakland way. They used to have certain names and certain words.

'The original Crusader Raider uniform was predominantly red and white – the colours of our divisional rivals, the Kansas City Chiefs. It was a red cape, with a white uniform featuring the red cross on the front with the chainmail and a normal Raiders logo. Over the years, the uniform developed. It now has loads of silver and black patches from booster clubs all around the world: Sweden, Italy, Ireland, Germany, and obviously the States, Canada and Mexico. We've gone through two electric sewing machines at home getting these patches on. The reworked shield on my chest was designed by a Raiders fan from New York, who added the words Crusader Raider above the team logo and created a custom-made patch which went on to the chest. Then silver and black ribbon was added to the red cape to give it a more appropriate border.

'After the first few years of going to games wearing this there were still a few people who would foolishly call me out. People would stand up for me in the Coliseum. Many times I thought there could be a fight or at least an argument because people defending me would say: "You should know who this is by now!" As you can imagine, after all those years of going to games in character most people know who I am.'

One person who didn't know who Crusader Raider was – at least initially – was Al Davis. The Raiders' patriarch crossed paths with Keith once and was shocked to see his colours. 'It was at the Oakland Coliseum when he was coming from his limousine,' says Keith. 'He was very ill in those later days, but he always would walk up the ramp towards the main entrance and talk to fans. He would be surrounded by security guards because he was really quite frail at that time. I went to shake his hand but sadly his security guards couldn't allow it because they needed to protect his health. We had a very brief conversation and a few days later I met his private secretary. I went to the team's facility in Alameda and she told me that I made a mark on Mr Davis. He couldn't understand who this crazy person was and why I would be wearing Kansas City Chiefs colours with a Raiders logo on the front of my chest. She had to explain the whole story to him about why I wear what I wear and then he understood. I was allowed to go into his office as long as I didn't take any pictures. Al obviously had his own bar, but he was teetotal so he had different Pepsi dispensers and things like that. He also had a colour chart to make sure that any piece of merchandise was the right tone of silver and black. There were samples that had been sent to him for approval because he approved everything personally.'

Keith talks about Al Davis with a fondness bordering on reverence due to the impact his creation of the Raiders ethos has had on his life and the lives of other fans across the UK. 'Mr Davis was very much about people and family,' says Keith. 'Back in Oakland, the lady who worked on the reception desk had been with the Raiders for 30 to 40 years, the same for his personal secretary. He used to give all the women on his staff necklaces to match the Super Bowl rings from the team's three Super Bowl victories. He appointed the NFL's first Hispanic head coach, the first black head coach, the first female CEO. He was very innovative. Would he have liked to stay in Oakland? Quite possibly, but I'm sure he would love to be in Las Vegas as well.'

As much as Keith feels Davis dedicated his life to doing the right thing by people, he himself has done the same. His work making sure that Raiders fans from outside the UK have enjoyed their trips to see International Series games has come before anything – even if it means missing out on the opportunity of a lifetime. 'When the Raiders played the Seahawks at Wembley Stadium in 2018 we put on a lot of events for visiting fans,' says Keith. 'We ran open-top bus tours, we organised a Jack the Ripper tour, we held pregame parties. We organised God-knows-how-many hotel rooms and Oyster cards for public transport access.

'The Friday morning before the game, while we were running the buses, I received a phone call from a representative of the Raiders asking me whether I would be willing to light Al Davis's torch at Wembley Stadium. The torch was originally at the Oakland Coliseum and it's now in front of the training facilities in Henderson, on the outskirts of Las Vegas. The team invites former players and coaches or celebrities to light the flame to keep the memory of Al Davis alive. They brought over a replica of the original torch and asked me if I could light it before kick-off. I was super excited and so was my daughter Kelly. And then I turned them down. I would have to come to a rehearsal and be at the stadium early but I'd already agreed to host and take 300 Raiders fans on the London Underground from Marylebone to the stadium. That was more important to me, which my daughter couldn't understand at the time, although I think she gets it a bit more now. I turned down one of the biggest honours – to light that torch for the Raiders in my hometown. But what was more important as a superfan or whatever anyone wants to call me, was ensuring that others were able to get to the game. I'd invited them to London and wanted to spend the morning with them, have brunch with them and get them to the stadium. But I do have a little bit of regret. Maybe I should have said yes, I don't know.'

Although he turned it down it's still a remarkable honour and a testament not just to Keith but to fan culture in the UK. No longer were UK fans considered simply a market and source of consumer spending, but an important part of making the sport what it is.

As well as being a die-hard Raiders fan, Keith is a soccer fan and season ticket holder at Leyton Orient FC so he decided to do some cultural exchange. 'Leyton Orient has American owners and the main owner is from Texas,' says Keith, 'but the chairman used to be the CEO of Dunkin' Donuts in the States and was born in Leytonstone. I got in touch with Leyton Orient and they hosted 70 Raiders fans, who were all in costume. They did a half-time penalty kick competition too. The Leyton Orient owners were in town that weekend and they came around to the sideline and shook the hands of every Raiders fan who had come in. It was great that I was able to help give fans from the States that experience because otherwise it wouldn't have been possible. I don't think a Premier League team's owners would have invited us into the supporters' club and given them all a free drink. One of the Raiders superfans who came to the match is a guy called Afro Deesiac and he has the biggest Afro wig going. His real name is Ken Webb and he is a cracking guy. After the match we walked down Leyton High Road and he couldn't resist walking into a barber shop and asking if there was any chance of a trim while he had his dirty great wig on. They said: "Unfortunately, we don't do that kind of hair."'

The Raiders superfans might have seemed like they had come from another planet when they walked through east London but when Keith becomes Crusader Raider he fits right in. Not only does he help spread the gospel of the NFL in the UK, he's also raised the profile of British fans in the US by becoming a celebrity in his own right. 'In 2014 the ice bucket challenge was a big thing [to raise money for ALS/MND],' says Keith. 'Dennis Allen, who was the Raiders head coach at the time, was filmed completing the challenge on the centre shield at the Oakland Coliseum. What you had to do then was challenge others to do the same. So he called out Gorilla Rilla, who's my good friend, and me! I had to do the challenge here in the UK, in my little garden in east London, in a paddling pool. When the team was in Oakland there used to be shows in the Bay Area and I was often invited on as a guest to tell the story of how football has developed outside the US. The Raiders have had both Menelik Watson from Manchester and Jack Crawford from London play for them so there is a strong connection on the playing side and this has meant American fans have developed an affinity with the UK. There was a time when I was out in the Coliseum car park and a huge truck was coming down the middle of the road. The driver was honking his horn and shouting for people to get out of the way. It turned out to be Menelik Watson making sure that he had the chance to say hello to me before he went into the stadium.'

Keith's profile in the US meant that in 2017 he became the first international fan to be drafted into an organisation called the Pro Football's Ultimate Fans Association [PFUFA]. The PFUFA celebrates superfans and the work they do to help communities. 'Each NFL team gets to nominate one fan per year for consideration and the Raiders chose me,' says Keith. 'It started with online interviews and the 32 fans were whittled down to 16. The next step in the process is a trip to Canton, Ohio, for a week-long interview of sorts. It's like a working interview where you interact with the community so the PFUFA can see more about your charitable work, how you support sportsmanship and deal with people. They voted for me to be accepted and I've been a proud member ever since.

'I go to Canton each year ahead of the annual Hall of Fame Game and with other PFUFA members we try to do things that will benefit the Canton community and those in nearby areas such as Akron, where people are really struggling. We spend a whole day at the J Babe Stearn Community Center in Canton working with families and children to provide everything from school supplies to bikes and computers, then have a barbecue and spend time with the people who have come in during the day. We also get involved in something called First Play, which is when a football is passed between all the schools in the Canton area. The football is then used in the first play of the Hall of Fame Game, which is the first game of the NFL preseason. That football gets passed through McKinley Park where we entertain the kids who have turned out, have photos taken, hand out cards and present gifts. I don't know what customs officers thought of me in 2018 when I took 300 Union Jacks in my suitcase. I signed every single one of them to give out to kids in Canton. I wanted to promote the fact that the NFL is worldwide and that fellowship among sports fans is worldwide. I don't wear the costume every day when I'm in Canton, but I still have the persona of Crusader Raider every day.'

The annual trips to Canton have become a highlight in Keith's year. When he is there he is always doing what he can to represent UK fans. 'For the PFUFA event, the tradition is that you decorate your hotel door to represent your team,' says Keith. 'I like to represent my country as well. One year I had the royal family on a balcony. My next one will have Tower Bridge and you can lift our bridge up and see Crusader Raider and Crossbones Kelly.'

If you don't know who Crossbones Kelly is, she's another Raiders superfan. She also happens to be Keith's eldest daughter. 'She's definitely followed in my footsteps as a superfan,' says Keith, 'and will be the future once Crusader Raider is well and truly gone. She's very lucky though because in the 1990s one of my favourite players for the Raiders was Napoleon Kaufman. He is now an ordained minister and was team chaplain of the Raiders for a while. Kelly would have been called Napoleon had she been a boy, so she got off lightly. My youngest daughter Kerry, who was born seven years later, was named after my favourite London Monarchs cheerleader. This was purely because she was a very good dancer and I was always impressed by the accuracy of her moves – no other reason. Kerry became a Miami Dolphins fan while Kelly followed in my footsteps. When the Raiders played the Dolphins in London in 2014 Kerry decorated the outside of the house with Dolphins gear. She almost got evicted that day.'

Keith may have a costume but it's nothing compared to the commitment his daughter needs to get into character each time she becomes Crossbones Kelly. 'I can get dressed in five minutes on game day,' says Keith, 'but it takes Kelly an hour because she paints her face and neck. One time we went to Tampa to watch the Raiders play the Buccaneers. It was a scorching hot day and we were getting ice out of the beer sellers' trays just to put on our necks and faces to keep cool. In the third quarter they stopped selling drinks – no water, no soda, nothing. The Raiders won in overtime so we were there in the heat for a long time. Our outfits were stuck to us like glue. Kelly has chains and skulls and God knows what else on her costume but her face paint was just melting away.

'When we got back to the hotel, Kelly washed her face paint off and we went in the pool to cool down. We soon realised that where the sun had been beating down it left the outline of the painted-on teeth and scars on her face. She had to spend two or three days trying to get enough sun to even out her face. People think the costume is what makes someone a superfan but that's not the case. Can you recognise a superfan out of his or her uniform because of what they contribute to football or the fellowship of fans or sportsmanship or charity? That's what counts. The outfits are just an add-on that you can put on at the end. If you recognise the fan for only their outfit, are they really a superfan? Or are they a super dresser?'

No one is going to confuse Keith with simply being a super dresser. He has become the best-known British fan in the US because of his actions rather than his outfit. Raiders fans are famous – some might say notorious – for their gameday costumes so just getting dressed up won't make you stand out. If the fact he was invited to light Al Davis's torch and called out by the team's head coach didn't make it obvious that he has become part of the fabric of the Raiders, the relationships he has with some one of the franchise's on- and off-field legends should seal the deal. When Gorilla Rilla (AKA Mark Acasio) got married to Jungle Jane (a Raiders superfan whose real name is Marilyn) it was covered by the media and got a big feature on the Raiders website. 'I was in the groom's party at that wedding,' says Keith. 'It was in Fresno, California in blazing heat and we were all in costume. A crazy wedding.'

Over the years Keith has also formed a close friendship with former Raiders' Hall of Fame wide receiver and Super Bowl XI MVP Fred Biletnikoff. 'I first got to meet Fred and his wife Angela back in 2004 in the car park of the Coliseum,' says Keith. 'They've been to my house and cooked on my barbecue while we watched a Raiders–Jets game on TV. They were over here visiting their daughter, Dacia, who studied for three years at London Contemporary Dance School. We were like her adoptive family over here. Not long after I met Fred and Angela I started supporting their foundation, which helps women who have suffered because of drug abuse or abusive partners. Apart from two years affected by Covid, I've gone to California every year to help their foundation and meet some of the women who are being helped. Here in the UK, I've had the opportunity to help our booster club raise funds for the foundation as well.'

The NFL's superfans do a tremendous amount of work to help good causes although most coverage will inevitably focus on their outfits. For Keith, he used clothes to promote the UK when he took it upon himself to help homeless people in the Bay Area. 'There's a group in Oakland called the 66th Mob,' says Keith, 'which was based on 66th Street – the opposite end of the Coliseum from the entrance to the car park. The 66th Mob does a lot to support the people who are struggling throughout the Bay Area. I used to go out with them to feed the homeless. We'd stay out all night, we would barbecue and provide supplies. I used to take warm blankets, scarves and hats. A few weeks after the London Olympics in 2012 you could get lots of London Olympics memorabilia really cheap. I bought up every colour and style of beanie hat at bargain basement prices. You would see homeless people in the Bay Area wearing London beanies more than any other hat because I bought so many.'

Keith's commitment to what he considers to be the main pillars of superfandom earned him a prestigious honour in 2019. 'I was awarded the Fellowship of Fans award for being the fan who had shown the most amount of fellowship in terms of welcoming people to stadiums and interacting with them in their cities,' says Keith. 'That award had never left the US before. I was awarded it for the work I had done in London. It's been wonderful to take US fans to places such as Tower Bridge or out into the country to see a castle where Anne Boleyn lived or the Imperial War Museum. I always say to people, when I'm going to Vegas, the game is just three and a half hours on a Sunday. I'm there for a week. What we do in that time as ambassadors is hugely significant. I think there should be a UK ambassador for every NFL team, but it's got to be someone who's doing it for the right reasons. It's about the fact that you've got a passion for your team and the sport, and you can promote the British fanbase around the world.'

Keith is obviously only doing things for the right reasons. He turned down the chance to light the flame because he didn't want to let other fans down. He's become famous in fan circles but it just means he has more responsibilities. Is being a superfan a blessing or a curse? 'It's an honour,' says Keith, 'it can never be a curse. I've never done anything to get something back. I've never ever said: "I'll come to Canton every year but you've got to pay for my flight or hotel." Everything I do, I pay for it myself. We're not the wealthiest family in the world but we enjoy the life we've got. It's not a chore. It's not hard work. It's just a bit challenging at times.

'Whenever I walked around the Coliseum car park before a game I would always be offered alcohol. I would never even take a sip until after the game because I was always aware of the fact that I would end up having pictures taken with other fans, very often children and families. I didn't want the slightest smell of alcohol on my breath because it is important to protect the character and identity of Crusader Raider. A superfan has to take responsibility for doing the right thing.

'Nothing is better in life than friends. I think you recognise that more when you look at the pandemic and how many people were alone. I never felt alone during the pandemic because of family and the huge NFL family around the world. During lockdown, we organised Crusader Raider colouring competitions and word searches for kids who were stuck at home isolated and bored. So when I think of things like that I know that the life of a superfan is a magical life if you embrace it. If this was my job or I got paid, I don't think I'd get the same kick out of it or have the same enthusiasm. I love the Raiders and I love the NFL. But I also absolutely love my American football family. We are a family and we are all connected.'

The lapsed fans return

IF IT wasn't for the fact that he's a familiar face on TV for Super Bowl broadcasts, Nat Coombs could be the person most fans of a certain age relate to. Started watching in the 1980s, drifted away a bit in the 1990s, threw himself back into it in the mid-2000s. But there's more to the story than that, of course.

'American football found its way into my consciousness through my innate love of America, which stretches as far back as I can remember,' says Nat. 'I was completely sports-mad as a kid in the 1980s and that was fundamental. I was interested in any sport. So a new sport that came along would grab my attention anyway but the Americana element of it made sure it stuck.'

Nat's gateway drug was the New York Jets' 51-45 victory over the Miami Dolphins in 1986, broadcast on Channel 4 on 28 September. Ken O'Brien and Dan Marino combined for a then-record 927 passing yards in what was one of the most dazzling games of the decade. As an advertisement for the sport there was probably nothing that could top it. 'Like so many of my generation, I watched those highlights not knowing really what the hell was going on,' says Nat. 'But I was completely captivated. It was intoxicating and I became a fan instantly. That set me off on a journey to understand the sport more. I was piecing things together from the commentary, but obviously there was very little room in those weekly highlights shows for analysis. So then it was down to all the additional things I could get my hands on, which meant any book that I could find in WH Smith and of course *First Down* when they came on the scene.'

The fact that fans nowadays can access so much NFL content on-demand is obviously a positive but Nat feels that the pre-internet days when most people in the UK only had four TV channels to choose from helped create the ideal environment in which the NFL could thrive. 'I think what was instrumental in me developing such an interest in the game was the fact that exposure to different worlds, people and environments was far more limited in the 1980s,' he says. 'So when you did find something by stumbling across it, it felt special. I was talking to my sister Beth about this recently because on a Friday night we would watch whatever film was on at 10.30pm after the news or whatever. That's what was on so that's what you watched unless you'd already gone out to rent a video. You can discover a lot of things that you wouldn't necessarily have given more than a second's thought to when your options are limited.'

Nat was hooked. He was watching the highlights, playing *John Madden Football* on his Commodore Amiga computer and if having the TV on to watch the Super Bowl all night wasn't an option, he'd turn to Armed Forces Network. 'It's one of the reasons I've got a real affinity with sports on the radio and particularly NFL on the radio,' he says. He would devour newspaper coverage of the sport, particularly in *The Times* (he is now a *Times* columnist). In the school playground he'd organise games among friends and make himself the quarterback – even going so far as to note down his completion and touchdown stats afterwards. ('I know this makes me sound like a geek,' he admits.)

Things started to change when Nat moved to a different school. 'The American football in the playground stopped at that point,' he says. 'I still kept in touch with the sport loosely, but it gradually started to fade. Soon games were on Sky but I didn't have that. I remember going on a family holiday this one time, and it wasn't the first time I had been abroad but it kind of felt like it because we hadn't been on holiday for donkey's years. We stayed in these quite swanky hotels around Europe because my dad sort-of blew the budget on this trip. But a lot of the time I didn't want to leave the room because they had all the sports channels. I remember trying to stay behind because I was watching a Texas Tech game.'

American football isn't the only sport Nat broadcasts nowadays and soccer was his first love. However, he draws parallels with his interest in the NFL fading and the fact years later he stopped playing soccer. 'I stopped for a really long time,' says Nat, 'and then only started again when I did my coaching badges, which I only did because I wanted to coach one of my kids' teams. I asked myself: "Why am I not playing any more?" I loved playing and don't know why I ever stopped. So I put a team together with some mates and we now play twice a week. Crucially, I can't imagine not doing it now. The fact I ever stopped seems completely irrational to me. It's not as if I stopped enjoying it. I just drifted away from it. And the NFL was a similar thing. I didn't fall out of love with it. I didn't get bored with it. It was just that other things distracted me. Before I knew it I became a lapsed NFL fan.'

For Nat, much of it came down to access. The best coverage was on Sky and he didn't live somewhere with a subscription. In the 1990s you couldn't easily read what the top US writers had to say or see American shows either. 'If there had been podcasts, subscription sites, such as The Athletic or the whole development of Substack writing, it might have been different,' he says. 'Nowadays you can get hold of so much. Without those things in the mid-to-late 1990s through to the early 2000s it was easy for the NFL to fade away for some people.'

Nowadays Nat is one of the most prominent podcasters as well as broadcasters in the NFL UK community, something it would have been hard for him to comprehend early in the 2000s. Although he wasn't avidly following American football, he was still connecting himself to the US. 'There was this LA Dodgers top I used to wear a lot,' says Nat, 'and when I was doing my first stand-up comedy gigs in 2003 I would often wear a vintage Pittsburgh Steelers T-shirt. I wasn't even watching the NFL at that point in my life.'

No one who has watched or listened to Nat will be surprised to learn about his comedy background. It came from a love of performing that had started when he was in school. 'For a long time I thought acting was what I wanted to do,' says Nat. 'I acted a lot in school and afterwards. I was in a [BAFTA-nominated] film with Judi Dench. Because I had that performing bug I stumbled into stand-up when I was fresh out of university. I was trying to work out what I wanted to do because I didn't study drama at university, I read English and that paved the way for the journalistic side of what I do.

'I had to pay my way through university in London and worked pretty much full-time during the degree at publishing houses in a very junior capacity. I got to learn the ropes of that side of things before I got spat out the other side of it. I still didn't know what I wanted to be. I acted a little bit at university so that was on the table. But tellingly, I guess, I didn't want to give up everything to pursue it. I liked writing. I liked performing.'

Nat was working as a press officer when somebody suggested he try stand-up. 'There was a gang of us at this place who were all in our early twenties and working in our first proper job,' he says. 'We all got on well, especially someone called Jamie who I'm still really good friends with now. We would all just mess around with comedy ideas. Things like prank calls and creating characters. That was a formative comedic development for me. When somebody said to us that we should try stand-up, Jamie was absolutely horrified. However, it sounded quite interesting to me.'

The main comedic influences for Nat at the time all hailed from the US. His favourite was Denis Leary. 'That was a wildly unpopular choice because to most people he was seen as a bit of a hack,' Nat admits. 'In particular, some people suggest he's a plagiarist and ripped off Bill Hicks. All I know is Leary had a lot of original material that was brilliant. I saw his breakthrough show *No Cure For Cancer* when I was still at school, and it was a seminal moment for me. This helped push me into trying it myself years later. I kept on doing it and built a bit of momentum. I was with a whole generation of really good stand-ups who all started around the same time. I'm not being self-deprecating when I say they were exceptional natural-born stand-ups and I probably wasn't. I could keep up with them but I didn't have the extra level they had. We hear a lot of athletes and players who have an awareness where they think: "Yeah, I can handle myself in this sport, I'm at this level so obviously there's something about me." But then they find themselves training with someone like Lionel Messi and it's only then they understand their own level. There is a difference.'

While Nat grappled with how he could keep up with some of his peers, he was still getting positive attention and unknowingly taking steps that would bring him back to the NFL. 'My work was in an undeveloped phase,' says Nat, 'but one of the interesting things about how the whole game worked, at least back then, was you could get propelled pretty quickly, even if you were still in a very formative stage. A lot of the comedians I was working with back then showed immense talent at the time and have gone on to forge careers at the very top of their game – the likes of Rhod Gilbert, Greg Davies and Roisin Conaty. We were on the same bills and I was holding my own but I wasn't getting the same level of hype they were because, after all, they are some of the most exceptional stand-ups of their generation. It was like being with Patrick Mahomes!

'I would be performing at gigs and there would always be agents. Often after a show an agent would chat to you. There were three or four big agents who would sign live comedians at the time and get them working with broadcasters. They would maybe take on five of them a year. You can do the maths on that. And each year there's yet another wave of budding comedians trying to get noticed. Hundreds and hundreds of them. It's pretty tough to break out when you're on the open mic circuit because you're going up and down the country often performing in pubs to 15 uninterested people. It's heavy sledding but brilliant grounding. I put in a fair amount of legwork and eventually I got signed by an agent. What became apparent to me fairly early on in that process, is that a lot of people think: "Right, that's it, I've made it. My career is sorted." Although being signed by an agent is important, it's still just a small step on that journey. This started my path to broadcasting but I wasn't sure which route I'd go.'

NFL fans across the UK know exactly which path he ended up on but it was a winding road before his now-legendary first stint with Mike Carlson. 'I got lots of different opportunities to do different things,' says Nat. 'I realised that I didn't want to be doing live stand-up. Everything I learned from doing it was really good and I loved the live element in particular, but I wanted to do something else. I still liked being in environments where you just have to sink or swim. A lot of comedy opportunities came in and I was still writing a lot of comedy. I appeared on panel shows and that kind of stuff. I developed a radio series based on a character I created. I did a pilot for an ITV prank show, which was a huge amount of fun. I think they pitched it as "*The A-Team* meets *Ocean's Eleven*". It had a big budget but didn't get commissioned. I was doing some presenting as well but it didn't really resonate with me because of the subject matter. I almost ended up getting the *E4 Music* job. I was getting quite a lot of presenting opportunities. My agent called one day and said: "You like sports, don't you?" And I said: "Yeah, sure." They asked: "What do you know about the NFL? Do you know that much about American football?"'

Nat couldn't believe it. He told his agent it was his favourite sport growing up and that he'd be interested no matter what it was. It turned out that it was the biggest gig in terrestrial NFL coverage – hosting live games on Channel 5 alongside Mike Carlson. Incumbent host Colin Murray was moving on and there was an opportunity for a fresh face if they had the NFL credentials. 'They don't want a conventional presenter,' says Nat. 'They wanted someone a little bit different to follow Colin, because he was a little bit different himself. The agent asked me if I would be interested in screen testing. Luckily I already knew the production company because I'd made a poker show with them. They screen tested me along with a bunch of other people, and although the production company has a bit of influence, of course, it's ultimately the channel that has the final say.'

Channel 5 picked Nat and started off a partnership between him and Mike Carlson that became the most iconic and enduring in the NFL's UK broadcasting history. It wasn't always easy, however. 'I was basically learning on the job,' he admits. 'I'd done all that stand-up but nothing prepares you for presenting on live television. The NFL is obviously a heavy-lifting live gig because you're on air a lot thanks to the breaks in the US broadcasts. It certainly was a baptism of fire that first year. But the thing is, within about 30 seconds of that first show, even though I was internally terrified and a bit lost in terms of actual technique, I knew this is what I was meant to be doing. I had complete conviction that this was my path. All the years being a fan of the NFL, along with the time spent acting, writing comedy and performing came together for that job. It just made sense. I wanted to be anchoring live sport. And in particular, live American sport.'

Live TV can be incredibly challenging and unforgiving. Especially for the NFL because you know your audience will include a mix of experts and newcomers. The key is preparation. 'The work I did before getting the NFL job gave me some miles on the clock as a performer,' says Nat, 'but I was still very new as a live presenter. The step up to cover a sport regularly, and therefore the journalistic leap that's required to do that, doesn't happen overnight. From day one, I was focused and I grafted. What was really important to me was the preparation and thinking about what viewers would want to know. You would always rather be over-prepared. Take a live International Series game in London on the BBC. I will have way too much material to talk about when I do those games so lots won't get used. Sometimes that really helps you out. There was a time a few years into the gig when Mike and I were doing one of the late-night games and it was hit by an electrical storm. The game was delayed by well over an hour. We had to fill so much time in the studio. Thankfully I was well-prepared for that show because

I'd been putting in the work ever since I got the gig and never let up.'

The first year that Nat and Mike were covering *Monday Night Football* together was 2007 – which after Channel 4's debut in 1982 and the breakthrough of the Chicago Bears in 1985, was perhaps the most pivotal in the sport's UK history. It was the year the NFL would play its first regular season game in the UK. Channel 5's show was the only place to watch live games on TV for free so Nat knew there would be a lot of curious newcomers wanting to see more of this intriguing sport. 'Every good host needs to make sure what they are doing is inclusive and that everyone's along for the ride,' says Nat. 'The style and approach can change, depending on whether you're doing say, a live International Series game from Wembley on the BBC rather than a late night show on Channel 4 or Channel 5 or a live radio show on talkSPORT compared with a podcast. But there needs to be a welcoming atmosphere because if someone is stumbling across the sport for the first time – like many people who grew up in the 1980s did on Sunday afternoons – you don't want them to feel like they're on the outside looking in.

'I know it's understandable but some presenters find it really important to show how much they know. I think that can be a mistake. It's true there is a very literate fanbase in the UK that is not going to suffer fools gladly if they think someone is oversimplifying it. That can alienate them. If you make the more dedicated fans feel patronised they're going to switch off. But from experience I think when you're hosting and you handle it right, you use the experts alongside you – such as Mike Carlson, Jeff Reinebold, Jason Bell, Osi Umenyiora and Phoebe Schecter to name a few – to handle most of the analysis and opinion. That will hopefully lead to lively, intelligent and engaging debate or discussion. Doing the late-night live games on Channel 4 and Channel 5 helped nurture the idea that we're all up together watching this, we're all part of the crew. Me, Mike and everyone else watching.'

Nat's chemistry with Mike has meant they've now been working together for more than 15 years. However, Nat says some of the credit for this should go to Colin Murray. 'A fair amount of the groundwork had already been laid by Colin,' says Nat. 'Colin only did it relatively briefly but because he's a brilliant creative mind, he set up a lot of the foundation. The "Ask Mike" segment we created, where viewers could send in questions about absolutely anything, was hugely popular. Colin had done something the season before on the theme of "things you didn't know about Mike Carlson" and he'd found stuff about Mike playing college football and things that paved the way for how I've done shows with Mike ever since. Colin showed you could talk about more than just football and we took it to that next level. Colin doesn't get enough credit for his role within all of this. Same goes for those behind the scenes. Producers and directors all have a really big part to play. If you've enjoyed a UK NFL broadcast, a lot of it is down to them, not just the people you can see on camera.'

The shows with Nat became the perfect opportunity for fans to see another side to Mike and allow Nat to bring his own lifelong passions of American pop culture and the NFL together. 'Mike seems to know everything about everything,' says Nat. 'He can just draw on a huge and credible knowledge base to make references and connections. This was important because we wanted to keep things light at times. We might come back to the studio for a US ad break and I would notice that one of the coaches looked like McNulty from *The Wire*, for example. From there we'd talk about who else from *The Wire* would make a good coach. You have to be careful to not overdo that. It's a little bit like Tony Romo predicting play calls. Initially everyone thought it was incredible. The more it happened the more people started to say it was getting tiresome. We always kept that balance. One minute Mike was explaining what happened on a key play, the next he's answering a viewer's question about what his favourite Bruce Springsteen album was.'

The timing of the show wasn't just good because of the launch of the International Series. It also came about while technology was allowing fans to connect in new ways. 'The years that we did that show together on Channel 5 and Channel 4 coincided with the onset of social media,' says Nat. 'People could get in touch with us easily during a live show. They created a Mike Carlson Appreciation Society on Facebook. Eventually they did one for me. I was really chuffed about that. They called it something like "Don't Worry, Nat, Here's Your Facebook Group", but hey, I'll take it! Later we would see that the show would be trending on Twitter while it was on. That was all down to the community who rallied around the show.'

During this time Nat became the voice of UK fans. Not by pushing his opinions but by asking all the right questions. Digging more into the game on live terrestrial TV, inviting new fans in, allowing the long-time fans to get closer to the game. It helped shape how a generation of fans consumed the sport. Nat was soon at the forefront of the podcast revolution, initially with Americarnage (made with Mike, plus Dan Louw and Harry Holgate), dedicated to the intersection between American sports and pop culture. The NFL's UK fans are now spoiled for choice when it comes to both homegrown podcasts and ones from the US. Around The NFL, the league's most prominent official podcast, is a big enough deal in the UK for the show's stars to be regulars on British TV. One of the line-up, Gregg Rosenthal, is also a frequent guest on The Nat Coombs Show podcast and told Nat something that changed his perspective on how he thought about the sport.

'I was doing a show with Gregg and he said, in an off-the-cuff way: "I'm not an Xs and Os guy so I spoke to somebody who's more of an Xs and Os guy." He said this openly on the podcast,' says Nat. 'I asked him about this because I also didn't really feel like I was a massive Xs and Os guy. And he was happy to admit to me: "Oh, no, I never have been, you know." Then I heard Peter Schrager [best known for NFL Network's *Good Morning Football* and for hosting his own NFL-backed podcast] say the same thing. He said: "I'd love to be an Xs and Os guy but I'm just not." And these are two of the very best NFL journalists in the US.

'Then I saw there's nothing wrong with saying there's still plenty about the game you don't understand. They don't act like that's their area of expertise and nor do I. That doesn't mean we don't have a good knowledge of the sport. You shouldn't pretend to be something you're not. I was always told to not worry too much about any criticism I got and equally don't believe the hype. I was always very happy asking what I felt were the right questions. Some people thought that meant I didn't know what I was talking about. Fair enough, that's their prerogative. I'm going to keep on feeding my brain and learning more by asking questions. With Mike, lots of the viewers will have questions they'd like to ask him. I'm just lucky enough to be the one to be able to ask him on a regular basis.'

Anyone who faces the glare of the media spotlight is destined to face some criticism, and Nat is no stranger to it, although from covering a variety of sports he's learned there are key differences between fans of other games. 'I've covered a fair amount of soccer during NFL seasons but in recent years I've backed away from that because I wanted to concentrate more on American sports,' Nat says. 'Soccer media has a very different vibe. I was hosting a show on talkSPORT and the topic of an incident during a Liverpool match came up. It was a Monday show and even the most die-hard soccer fan, let alone broadcaster or journalist, wouldn't claim to have watched every single second of every Premier League match each weekend. On the show I said I'd only watched the highlights of that game so hadn't seen the incident but a friend of mine is a Liverpool season ticket holder and told me something interesting about it. Twitter blew up within seconds. Fans were saying: "Get this presenter off the air! He didn't even watch the full game. What a joke!" Meanwhile, the NFL's UK community is definitely more supportive and friendly. But – and it's a big but – you can't parachute someone in who doesn't have either a passion for the sport or a knowledge of the game. They can smell a phoney a mile off.'

The years that Channel 4 and Channel 5 broadcast live games helped drive huge growth for the NFL in the UK. However, the only way to watch the biggest game of the week is to pay for Sky Sports or NFL Game Pass, which disappoints Nat. 'I think it's a massive mistake to not have *Sunday Night Football* on terrestrial,' he says. 'And I know it's not as simple as one person deciding it should happen; there are a huge number of things that need to join up for that to happen. What 5 have done with *Monday Night Football* is great. I love the way they use Gregg Rosenthal in particular. The impact of access to live games each week is underestimated. I think the NFL is missing a trick by not having the next-gen version of me and Mike on that show talking to the hardcore group and the curious new fans.'

Nat's coverage of the NFL is everywhere but the thing he enjoys the most is his weekly radio show on talkSPORT covering all the 6pm games as they happen. Why? Because it's the broadcast that makes him feel most like a fan. 'It's like watching it with mates,' says Nat. 'I love working on it. There's nothing that beats sitting back in a bar with friends or at home with my kids watching the games. The radio show is like that. Deep down I am simply a fan. Over the years I've become more accomplished as a broadcaster and I'm better at what I do. But the cornerstone of the Sunday NFL stuff I do is driven by the fact that I'm just like everyone else watching this at home. We're the same. We're the people who would be up at 3am to watch Carson Palmer simply because we love this sport.'

Fantasy football creates a new audience

THE RISE of the NFL in the UK from 2010 onwards cannot be disconnected from the rise in fantasy sports. During this decade the number of regular players taking part in fantasy NFL competitions skyrocketed. In the 2020s much of the growth has come from people playing daily fantasy to win cash, a game arguably more in line with traditional gambling than the games that focus on groups of friends playing head to head for bragging rights over the course of a season. It's this 'friendly rivalry' element that has been the biggest fantasy factor in helping the NFL take such a significant foothold in the British sporting landscape. The ease with which fans from across the UK can communicate with one another and compete in the same league has been a key entry point for new fans. But before this boom there was a small group of British pioneers who wanted to go deep inside these games, share their expertise and encourage others to get on board.

'Growing up I was aware of American football because of games on various computer platforms and whatnot,' says Neil Dutton. 'I knew what a *John Madden Football* game was but I couldn't have told you anything about it. When I was about 18 or 19 my friends and I were always going out drinking beer but for 20 weeks at the end of the year some of them just stopped coming out on a Sunday. It was OK, because there were plenty of us still out there. It didn't really matter. Then there were a few Sunday nights where no one else was going out. So I was faced with the dire prospect of not being able to go out at all, or finding someone, anyone, to accompany me. So I asked them, "What are you doing? Why aren't you coming out?"'

If you're reading this book you probably already know what Neil's friends were doing on a Sunday evening. However, back in 2000, when the sport was at a low ebb in the UK, it wouldn't have occurred to most people outside the small NFL community.

'They said: "We're watching the NFL,"' remembers Neil. 'So I said: "Well, OK, I'm not really that interested in the NFL but can I come round and watch with you?" Which to me meant "Can I come and sit with you while I drink a few beers?" The first game I watched was the Jets against the Dolphins on 19 November 2000. I had to go back and do some research years later to figure out when the game was but I remembered the teams because one of my mates was a Jets fan. It was back in the days where we usually only had one live Sunday game on Sky Sports and that week it was on at 9pm. Dolphins quarterback Jay Fiedler got knocked out of the game on the first play and it went downhill for the Dolphins from there. I was watching it but I was "in my cups" as they say.'

So Neil was enjoying the social side of the sport, and the chance to have a few beers, but the game itself wasn't grabbing him. Yet. 'At the time it just looked like big buggers banging into each other,' he says. 'The next week I was asked if I wanted to come along again, so I did. And then I went a few more times. As I started watching more, I started taking less alcohol with me. That way I could actually watch the game and start asking questions about it.'

Since then Neil hasn't stopped asking questions, trying to figure out why things have happened and what it means for how games will pan out and how players will perform the following week. But before it started to take over his free time he had to power through and watch a Super Bowl, a watershed moment for him.

'I was used to a live game starting at 9pm, finishing around midnight, and then you can just go home, get up and go to uni or go to work the next morning,' says Neil. 'The Super Bowl started at 11.30pm and finished at God-knows-what time. Because I stayed up for that and enjoyed it, that was the first time I realised I was properly into it. I knew this wasn't just going to be a casual dalliance. As soon as the game was over I asked my mates: "OK, when's the season starting?" When they told me it was September I remember thinking it was a long time to wait and that maybe I won't bother. However, as it got closer, and my friend was getting his weekly copy of *First Down*, I was getting more excited. That's when I started realising this is something I'm genuinely going to be interested in now, this isn't just something I did because I had nothing else to do. Incidentally, to get *First Down* we had to go into a town about six miles away from where we lived, because that was the only place that we could find a copy.'

Although Neil was now a fan, his fandom was tied in very closely to the social aspect of watching games with friends. 'For the first decade I was watching it I would always go to watch it at someone else's house because friends of mine had back rooms in their homes, somewhere they could watch the NFL without getting in their family's way. I'm not taking a shot at my parents but they did only have one big room for watching TV. I couldn't banish them to another house just because I wanted to watch the NFL. Gradually things happened, such as Mainzy [Paul Mainwaring], who is now my esteemed podcast co-host, moved away for work and another one of my mates got married. Eventually I realised I would have to watch it by myself now. By that time I was

32 and although before then it was all social, I would have happily watched it by myself if I'd had the opportunity.'

An aspect of the social side of the sport for Neil was playing fantasy NFL games with his friends. Although he first started doing this in 2005, he'd initially played the Premier League soccer version in the 1990s. This was inspired by Frank Skinner and David Baddiel's hit BBC TV show *Fantasy Football League*, itself a spin-off of a radio version that tapped into the growing popularity of fantasy soccer in the UK. 'That was the show that got me interested,' says Neil. 'At the start it clearly focused on the fantasy side of things. It eventually became a lot more about the comedy and the guests. It was those early episodes that made me realise: "Oh, I see, so even though that player didn't score a goal they can still score points for it." I found a computer program that let me make my own leagues, which I used to become commissioner of my own fantasy Premier League. I would watch *Match of the Day* every Saturday so I could see who got the assists and who was playing in defence. I would sit there with a pen and a pad desperately hoping I could see who crossed the ball or who played the final pass. And then on Sundays and Mondays I'd watch the live Premier League games the same way to log the points. I did it all myself so it could be as accurate as possible. And then being a Sheffield Wednesday fan, I fell out of love with that sport.'

At the end of the 1999/2000 season, Neil's beloved Sheffield Wednesday were relegated from the Premier League. Just eight years earlier they had finished third in England's top soccer division. 'I'm from Liverpool,' says Neil, 'but my granddad was a Sheffield Wednesday fan and a proud Yorkshireman. He was the only one of his family who supported Wednesday because the rest supported Sheffield United. He died in 1992, so being the hero that I am, I –

along with my sister – decided to support Wednesday. In the first year I supported them they reached two cup finals at Wembley. After they were relegated my interest in the sport itself really started to wane.'

At this point Neil had no idea that his deep interest in the mechanics of fantasy soccer and the strategy of American football would come together in such a significant way. 'I already liked the idea of fantasy sports and I knew how it would work in the NFL,' says Neil. 'Sky Sports would make references to fantasy teams on their NFL shows but it was essentially 'best ball' [a format where you draft a roster of players but don't set a weekly line-up, it's done automatically after the fact depending on who scored the most points]. At the time I didn't think that was interesting. While I was young and naive back in the day I was always convinced there were too many stats in the NFL. Even after watching the NFL for five years I didn't realise the strategy that went into the fantasy version when we first started it.

'The first year I played was the season after the Philadelphia Eagles had reached Super Bowl XXXIX. Therefore the Eagles must be really good. So I drafted Donovan McNabb with the fourth overall pick and just decided: "Yeah, I'm set." Of course, he ended up getting injured and missed most of the season. At this point I was just desperate to not finish last in the league so I was committed to changing my team on a weekly basis. One of my mates was a bit sharper than me. So he made sure that if there was a good player available on the league's waiver wire he wasn't there for long, he was on his roster very quickly. In the kingdom of the blind, the one-eyed man is king. He made sure the rest of us were down and stayed down.'

It just goes to show that everyone has to start somewhere. Years later Neil would be paid to share his fantasy NFL expertise with the world but it was a slow process. 'For two or three seasons I just played in one league,' says Neil. 'A few people dropped out and we replaced them. A few other people in work started getting interested as well. Soon I was in a few leagues but only two or three. As time went on I started talking to [radio and podcast presenter] Will Gavin and [writer] James Dixon through social media. And the more connected you seem to people like that, the more people start inviting you to join their leagues. Most of my fantasy journey wouldn't have been possible if it wasn't for Twitter. That's how I started finding out about podcasts, started listening to people, conversing with them on that, and getting invited to do things. Then I started looking at the fantasy world a bit more. I thought: "I don't just want to do this, I want to do it well." I realised I needed to start reading about how to get better at it, figure out how to go into the draft with a plan.'

Reading turned to writing for Neil, and if the world of American football and its fantasy games were initially alien to him, writing certainly wasn't. This was something that he'd loved for a long time and his family were fully behind it. 'My mum always wanted me to write and that goes back to when I was in school,' says Neil. 'She always felt that I had a talent for writing. I suppose I did have talent but the real question was how to use it because I didn't have anything to write about. That changed in the 2012 season when I saw an advert on Twitter for a site looking for NFL writers. So I sent off a few pieces. They were happy for me to join them. After that the site was tweeting out links to stories with my name on it so I started connecting with people on other sites and podcasts based in the UK.'

Playing fantasy NFL changed Neil's relationship with the game dramatically and his tale is not unique. Not everyone pours as much time and effort into analysing fantasy potential but it's a huge factor in getting eyes in the UK on American football. Neil has just one regret. 'I think it was two weeks after my first daughter was born that I started writing about fantasy NFL,' he says. 'It was the worst possible moment to start doing it. I should have started in the first few seasons I was watching. I could've done some scribbling and asked some people for advice. I had no major attachment or financial obligations back then. Mummy and daddy looked after me, bless them. I could have tried to pursue it as a career although the opportunities to make a career out of it didn't really exist when I was 20. When opportunities arrived I was in my 30s and already had commitments. I couldn't just go off to LA to try my luck. My missus said she would have kicked me out.'

The thing with writing about fantasy sports is that your readers are invested and if you give bad advice your audience will know very quickly. If you suggest people start Quarterback A over Quarterback B on a Sunday evening and Quarterback B has a much better game, people are going to let you know about it straight away. The pressure is real. 'I needed to make sure that what I was writing was actionable,' says Neil. 'And it wasn't just: "Oh, you should draft Peyton Manning." "Oh, gee, thanks. That's really helpful." It was more along the lines of what you can do if you can't take Peyton Manning. Once I started writing about it I really started focusing on actually getting better at it.

'There might be a few bad apples in the community but I like to think I have good relationships with a lot of people. I write for a large cross section of sites so I do have contact with people who will or won't follow particular websites because the owner of that site has championed a certain philosophy. Certain people aren't shy about expressing their opinions about a whole host of matters and they know it drives engagement. I'm lucky that my following is too small for anyone to "hate-follow" me. If there's something I embrace with my writing it's that I don't know everything. As much as I'd love to, I know I don't. It's like being a quarterback: if you know, and accept, you're going to get hit it won't hurt as much. If I accept I'm going to be wrong occasionally, it doesn't hurt any more.'

One of the key differences between a typical fantasy NFL league and a typical fantasy soccer competition is that the NFL version will feature head-to-head match-ups. No matter how many points you win or lose by in a single match-up, it's still simply a win or a loss in the standings. If you have a terrible few weeks at the start of a long fantasy soccer season that may completely rule you out of finishing first. Or at least demoralise you to the point where you stop checking your team every week and fail to make suitable transfers. In the NFL version everything is week to week. It's practically a clean slate at the start of each gameweek and the owner of a struggling team will at least know it's not about finishing with the most overall points, it's finishing high enough in the division to make the playoffs.

Just like in the NFL, your team could get hot at the right time and win a championship despite being mediocre for half a season. That won't happen in the real-life Premier League or the fantasy version. A new NFL fan from the UK playing in a fantasy league for the first time isn't likely to feel intimidated if the league they are in is as wide-open as most leagues are. They'll also end up using the experience to learn more about the players in the league and the role of different positions. They'll certainly watch a lot more games. And it's why there are so many games on TV now.

'We know players and coaches hate *Thursday Night Football* because it's a short week and there is an increased risk of injuries,' says Neil. 'Fantasy football is the reason games are played that night because people have then got a reason to sit there for say, Jacksonville vs Tennessee playing in hideous uniforms. The NFL can put a game on TV that night knowing people will watch due to the fantasy scoring implications. Someone in your league will have Ryan Tannehill, for example, and you might need him to have a good or bad game depending on who in your league you are trying to catch. If there was no fantasy NFL, then you're relying on the fans of those two teams and the most dedicated die-hard fan who will watch absolutely everything. Those two groups won't pay the bills – you need the fantasy football players.'

The biggest impact fantasy NFL has had on broadcasting isn't the addition of extra game slots though, it's the huge popularity of *NFL RedZone*, a seven-hour live show that features every score and big play across the league with no ad breaks. In the US there are two dedicated services. *NFL RedZone*, which is part of NFL Network and hosted by Scott Hanson; and NFL Red Zone Channel, which is part of DirecTV's premium Sunday Ticket package and is hosted by Andrew Siciliano. In the UK, only the NFL Network version is available and some UK fans who are trying to watch online via an illegal stream are often confused as to why Hanson has seemingly been replaced by Siciliano on a totally different set.

NFL RedZone is available in the UK on Sky Sports Mix and the NFL's own Game Pass streaming service. Crucially, viewers can watch Mix without a Sky Sports subscription and you don't need the top tier of Game Pass membership to watch it either. Not only is there less of a financial barrier to accessing *NFL RedZone*, it's also incredibly accessible to new fans. It's action-packed and will feature every single exciting thing that happens in games played between 6pm and 1am on a Sunday night (UK time). If you're an American who doesn't like the NFL, the show is unlikely to convert you. However, if you're a British fan who doesn't have the NFL on their radar but stumbles across *NFL RedZone* either accidentally or because friends are watching, then see the spectacular plays that happen minute to minute? That's a different story. Although the show is hugely important to the fantasy sports industry and that's why it has become so big, it's arguably more important in the UK as a recruitment tool. But is this reliance on fantasy points and spectacular highlights preventing newer fans from understanding the nuances of the sport?

'Speaking as someone who hates T20 cricket, I still know how valuable it is to get that sport to a new audience,' says Neil. '*NFL RedZone* is a great way to get people involved and I love Scott Hanson, but if it's all you watch, you're not going to get the full NFL experience. A full game isn't packed with 50-yard pass plays or huge interception returns. If you want to understand the intricacies of what's going on, you get more watching a drive of your own team than you will from *NFL RedZone*. Especially if the team you're a fan of isn't very good that season. If your favourite team isn't scoring many touchdowns this year you're not going to see them much on *NFL RedZone*.'

Neil isn't a typical fan, of course. He's become one of the most respected voices in the UK's fantasy NFL sphere so watches games in a particular way. It's probably a routine that many fantasy obsessives in the UK can relate to. 'I watch *NFL RedZone* on a Sunday then I will watch some condensed games on Monday. During the week I will try to watch as many of the other condensed games as possible. *NFL RedZone* is obviously perfect for fantasy because you're seeing all the touchdowns. And usually that's what drives fantasy football: who scored a touchdown, who's catching the passes, who's running the ball, who's passing the ball. It doesn't really focus on a great block by the right guard, or cover three rotations because it doesn't score fantasy points.

'I'm active on Twitter on a Sunday too. I see beat writers who tweet about their team during the game with just the word "wow". I need a bit more than that. I will send tweets about various different things that are happening in different games. I'll make sure I get the right hashtag in as well – you don't want to use the wrong hashtag. I just don't have time to watch as much as I would like so *NFL RedZone* helps my fantasy work because I can, for example, see that Jimmy Graham got targeted six times in the red zone for no apparent reason. I can use that information going forward.'

Unlike many fantasy die-hards Neil isn't obsessing about his scores the whole time but that's only because he's seen the downsides. 'At one time I probably had 15 teams in 15 different leagues and it felt like they were all on 15 different apps,' he says. 'If you've got 15 teams, you'll have some players on multiple teams but mostly it's 15 teams with totally different players. At that time I'd be looking down and checking my phone all the time on a Sunday. I realised: "I'm not watching this, I'm not watching the game." So my rule now is I don't look at my fantasy teams until the 9pm games are done.

'Playing fantasy also helps you get over the disappointment of your favourite team losing much quicker. You can focus on the next game starting in 20 minutes with one of your key fantasy players involved rather than falling into a pit of despair, thinking: "I can't believe the Eagles did that." Otherwise you might be in such a bad mood after a defeat in the early game that you think you'd rather go to bed than carry on watching. This is why the final week of the season can feel so futile. Most fantasy leagues will have wrapped up their seasons before then because so many teams rest their starters at that point. You don't get that nice fantasy distraction like you did for the rest of the regular season.'

The UK's fantasy NFL community has become a very welcoming place for new fans and a space where those who are writing and podcasting about it to a wide audience are supportive of one another. They're not just talking about a sport and a fantasy game they love, they're representing all British fans and fantasy players. Neil believes that most of his readers are American because they are more likely than British fans to subscribe to a fantasy site with a paywall.

'One massive difference that I noticed between our fantasy football players and those in the States is that Americans are far more likely to play for money,' says Neil. 'You'll always hear people on US fantasy NFL podcasts talking about paying league dues. They play with the aim of taking money off their schoolmates. In this country we still play it like, for want of a better phrase, an amateur pastime. So I think there are UK fans who pay for access to sites I write for such as Rotoviz and 4for4 but it will be mostly the US fans because they are actively trying to win money. Matthew Berry [US TV and movie screenwriter turned fantasy NFL guru] has written lots about the silly forfeits that the person who finishes in last place in leagues has to do. Things such as getting tattoos or walking around dressed in a nappy in public areas. It's incredible what these people are prepared to do because they know that next year they might win and it will be someone else doing this embarrassing thing.'

Another big difference that comes out of this is that Americans are routinely playing in leagues with people they know in real life whereas the typical UK fan is playing against like-minded fans they met online. As popular as the sport has become in the UK, most fans don't have a group of friends from school or work who are also die-hard NFL viewers and fantasy players. 'The Americans in their home leagues are generally surrounded by their buddies from high school or college,' says Neil. 'They will go to someone's house and have an in-person draft. The draft is a massive social event in those leagues, whereas in the UK the players in your league are possibly spread far and wide, and that's the same for the leagues I am in. There's me up in Liverpool and Mainzy down in Yarmouth for example. Because it's such an amateur pursuit for us in the UK, we're not all going to go to the expense of meeting in a central location to have an offline draft together.'

The American fans playing fantasy tend to be avid viewers already whereas many British players are just taking their first steps together. Planning ahead of a draft and making changes during the season is a great way to learn more about the sport. 'If you start watching the NFL, you want to know who the good players are. You might be introduced to a player through fantasy then decide that's the team you're going to follow. If you sit down with a new fan and say: "OK, what you're seeing in this play is that they've decided to slide protection left," they won't get it. But if you say: "He just ran 25 yards and that scored my team a point," the understanding will come.'

Much like NFL fans in the UK feel a certain level of kinship with others who have taken the sport to their hearts, the nation's fantasy community is the same way. They support one another and champion their hobby together. When Steve Raynes, a popular podcaster and voice within the fantasy community died at the age of 38, the community – led by his co-hosts Jack Humphrey and Jamie Byrom – rallied around to raise money. Their podcast was renamed Steve Raynes Fantasy Show and they now hold an annual fantasy competition in his name. 'I've been in the Steve Raynes Bowl charity tournament,' says Neil. 'There was a real outpouring when he died that seemed to bring everyone together because it was one of our own. It's good to remember someone who would love to have someone from the UK make it big in the fantasy world.'

NFL fans in the UK are still waiting for a British player to become one of the league's undisputed stars. Meanwhile, those active in the UK's fantasy community are hoping that one of their own can be one of the most prominent experts in the US and shine a light on the work that many others are doing. 'Everyone sees a version of their own NFL journey in other people,' says Neil, 'and we always want one another to do well. I would like to think in the next few years there could be a UK face on one of the major networks in the US talking about fantasy NFL.'

Community stars spread the love

'CAN NFL players stop nicking my Sharpies, please?' Claire Ball has a simple but unusual request. She appreciates how many stars have come to the UK to meet fans and sign autographs but is less appreciative of the way that they disappear with her pens. 'Take Andrew Luck,' she says. 'He's a multi-millionaire but walked off with not one but two of my Sharpies.' But how did Claire, better known to fans in the UK and around the world as Claire Da Bear, get to the point where she's always in front of NFL players handing them pens?

'It's a typical superhero origin story,' says Claire. 'It's a dark and stormy night. My mother is pregnant with my baby brother, Matthew. There is an age gap in our family between the older children and the rest of us. So the oldest children could stay at home, but I couldn't because I was three years old. I was bundled into the car with my pregnant mum and we went to the hospital. My dad wasn't in the room with her. Instead he sat outside with me and watched Super Bowl XX on the small hospital waiting room TV as the Chicago Bears beat the New England Patriots.

'My dad is a fan of Washington and we're a military household. I'm an army brat so that meant American sport was not unknown to us. We had plenty of American friends. To me the players looked like superheroes hitting each other and making lots of noise. I thought: "This is lots of fun and it's a very exciting sport to watch." C is the first letter of my name so it was a big deal at that age seeing that on the Bears' helmets. To make things even better they play in navy and orange which were – and still are to this day – my favourite colours. I didn't pick the Bears. The Bears picked me. It was like the clouds parted, the angels sang and the NFL came down and said: "I bless you, my child, you're now into the NFL. Enjoy that while you're overseas and suffer when you can barely get any access to the thing that you love for many, many years." I've been a long-suffering Bears fan ever since for my sins. Admittedly there are some mornings where I have regrets but I will stick with them. When I die, I want Bears players to carry me to the grave so they can let me down one more time. Until Mitch Trubisky I had never owned a Bears quarterback jersey. Even then it was simply because it was a special edition for the team's 100th anniversary. And I stand by that, your honour.'

The night baby Matthew was born, many NFL fans, and especially Bears fans, were born across the UK. It's arguably the most significant American football game in UK history, even though it was played thousands of miles away in New Orleans. If you meet NFL fans of a certain age you won't have to look hard to find Bears obsessives whose lives were changed by Super Bowl XX. In that way, Claire is no different. What makes her stand out are the things she has done since then to put the needs of the UK fan community (and fans much further afield) above her own. Claire has become the glue bonding together fans across the country when they can't get close to the sport they love.

'Obviously I was very young when that Super Bowl happened so there was only so much I could do,' admits Claire. 'Once I was in school, I was the only kid with a Kangaroos sweatband and a William Perry T-shirt. Eventually I had paper rounds to earn money so I could get my NFL fix. My dad had a VHS tape subscription service. You would pay your money and you would get sent a game. You couldn't pick what you got, you just got what was given to you. The games would come on two tapes because they were too long to fit on just one. You could then send the tapes back and earn credit towards your next one. Or you could keep your tapes and end up paying more money. Around this time I would get a copy of *USA Today* to check the results or spend ages scrolling through Teletext to find the scores. Obviously I used to listen to commentary on Armed Forces Network radio. I would have to tune my radio in – and I mean, really tune it in – to hear anything. I'd have to have my arm in a certain way or I would lose the signal. You needed the wind blowing in the right direction or you got nothing. It was like some sort of witchcraft. Sometimes I would listen to games and then the French shipping forecast would cut through. It always felt like this happened during a big play.

'I got grounded more than once for sneaking downstairs to watch the Super Bowl. Once when I got caught my dad said I could choose how long I was grounded for. I could be grounded for a month or be grounded for one day for every point scored in the game. I took the points total and it was a bad decision. All these mis-spent hours looking through newspapers, Teletext or tuning the radio made my fandom what it is today. It makes me love the sport all the more because of the effort I put in polishing the stone. It's like I was mining for something. I had to dig deep in the mine getting dirty. The gem I discovered, I didn't want to keep it to myself. I want to show the rest of the world through social media how shiny, beautiful and desirable it is.'

Eventually Claire was older and access to the sport she loved was easier. It was the creation of the official NFL UK online forum that turned her from a fan to a superfan. From

Claire to Claire Da Bear. 'I gave myself that name when there were not many women – and certainly not many Claires – on the site,' she says. 'That name stuck. I've had people call that name out to me in London even when I'm not dressed in my costume. Even my doctor refers to me as Claire Da Bear. It's confused my postman because people have sent me stuff for my giveaways and addressed it to "Claire Da Bear". I've had to go to the post office and explain who this superhero alter ego is because they tell me this person doesn't exist.'

Picking the name was easy and it goes back to her family. 'I have an older sister called Nicola,' says Claire. 'Her nickname is Yogi Bear. And Yogi Bear always gets the little bear Boo-Boo into trouble. That was very much our dynamic in my childhood. I've always been called Claire Da Bear. And I'll always be that person in some way or another. I'm wearing my fan costume now, even though I'm on my own and no one can see me. If I'm talking about this I have to be it.'

The NFL has many dedicated fans in the UK but few are as dedicated as Claire. Everything she does is to make things better for other fans. 'I want everyone to feel and enjoy the passion of the NFL,' says Claire. 'It's like I'm having a whale of a time at the NFL party and want everyone to join me on the dancefloor. It doesn't matter which team you support. As a Bears fan, when I see a Green Bay Packers fan I will boo them as I walk past. But it's a friendly panto-style boo.

'A close friend of mine, Susanna, is a referee here in the UK. I love American football so much that I will go with her to British games in the summer and winter just to get access to the thing that I love. I will work on chain crews for random teams throughout the season to be close to the sport. I think every UK fan should volunteer in the British leagues. There will be a job for you. Maybe you're an accountant – that could really help a team out. If you can't play, if you're not fit enough, don't think you've got the confidence, just volunteer.

'I'm a high-functioning autistic adult and one of the things I've struggled with is conflict. I know I can't be a referee because I know at some point I'll make a decision – the right decision – and someone's going to end up unhappy with me. I can't handle that. So the best thing I can do for the community and myself is volunteer on the chain crews. Doing that job I've seen some of the greatest plays ever but they will never be seen by a wider audience because there are no cameras there. There was one play where I had no idea how the ball got where it was – other than someone from *Star Trek* beamed the ball in. I've seen beautiful sportsmanship. I was on the sideline of a David vs Goliath-style match where the Goliath team played slowly as if it was practice and helped the David players off the ground. They knew if there was one more injury the game would be forfeited and no one wanted that to happen.'

Claire has become legendary within the NFL UK community. If there's a big event happening, chances are she is there. If there is a player signing autographs it's almost certain you will spot her holding a pen. 'I've done this a lot but one time was particularly memorable,' says Claire. 'In July 2019, the summer before the Bears came over to play the Raiders at Tottenham, the NFL did what they usually do and sent over a player from each team to do press and promotional events. I started queuing about eight hours before the event had started. They hadn't even got the posters up to say the event was on and I was there.

'Because I was one of the first 30 people in the queue I would get to meet the players, one of which was Akiem Hicks. Eventually I hear a booming voice that sounds like Santa Claus coming from the hallway. Holy crap. Then I felt a hug. I'm quite a big girl, so if I give someone a hug I'm the bread and they're the filling. Very few times have I had it where someone else is the bread and I'm the filling. When a player like Akiem Hicks hugs you, you definitely get to be the filling. He gave me a massive hug and said: "You're crazy! I could have flown from Chicago in the amount of time you stood out here waiting!"

'Ahead of the same game, Charles Tillman and Jim Plunkett were both in the UK as well. It was a very Bears-heavy crowd everywhere you went around that game so a lot of fans wanted to meet Tillman, and not as many wanted to meet the two-time Super Bowl champion Plunkett. Nothing was safe near Tillman. He just wanted to sign everything. I stood next to him with a Sharpie and he ended up signing my fan costume – which wasn't part of the plan. The lack of interest in Jim Plunkett worked really well for me because he was lovely and signed seven things for me. That meant seven Raiders fans who couldn't be there in person got something special.'

The reason that Claire will devote so much time and energy to waiting in line to get things signed is because she knows there are lots of people who wish they could do this but aren't able to for whatever reason. Almost every item she gets signed is given away to other fans. Over the years Claire has given away hundreds of items to fans across the world just to share her love of the game and make others feel connected to the NFL. 'I will always try to get as much time as possible so I can get some extra things signed,' she says. 'When I go to get autographs, it's not about me, it's about you. It's about the little boy in Scotland who can't afford to go to an NFL game in person. It's for the guy in Australia who knows the NFL might not play a regular season game in his country in his lifetime.

'I'm very lucky that the NFL courts London. I don't actually live in London, but when NFL UK says it's doing something in London I'm close enough that I can practically drop almost anything and run towards it. It's a bit like one of those scenes in a romantic movie where someone runs through the airport towards the one they love. When the Bears played the Raiders over here in 2019 I had things all planned out. I decided that whatever I got on Friday was going to be for Claire. But then Saturday and Sunday have to be dedicated to giveaways for other people. It can't all be for Claire. People know what I'm about and they know I'm a one-man band. I've had it where people will see me arrive at an event and they'll let me cut ahead of them in the queue because they know that way there will be more giveaways and more people get to keep a piece of signed merchandise.

'If you've ever donated anything to me for a giveaway, even if it's just a key ring, you've made a difference to someone else. If you've paid me back for postage or if you've had a clearout and sent me a T-shirt that someone else might like, that's been a massive help. I've had some winners tell me they had gone on holiday to the US and brought me back a present to give away. God bless you all, because the community has kept this going, not just me.'

One of the downsides of being famous within a community is that people impersonate you. There have been times when people have created Twitter accounts pretending to be Claire and sent messages to other users saying they have won a giveaway and asked them to send over personal details before their prize can be posted. Being a recognisable person in the community can be hard, even when people aren't trying to use your identity to scam other fans. Being 'public property' has taken its toll on Claire although she's battled through to make sure she can help the wider community. She couldn't have done it without her family.

'I have to genuinely thank my mum for letting her nerdy, chubby little girl be an NFL fan and not be pushed towards Barbie dolls instead,' says Claire. 'She also helped me design my fan costume. My sister supported me to become this superhero and take on this persona. She helped me put on this cape and be brave because the real Claire is shy and stuttering. When people ask what superpower I would like I always say invisibility. I want to not be a nuisance and be a "nothing person". However, Claire Da Bear doesn't want to be invisible. She wants to be seen from the Hubble telescope.

'I do know that when I go out in public and wear my costume, I become public property. Because of my autism I don't enjoy being touched. But I know that people will want to touch me, hug me and have lots of photographs taken with me. I'm well aware that's what will happen and I accept it. I use up so much energy going to games in London that it can take me up to two weeks to recover from a game. That's not due to alcohol because I won't be drinking. It's just the energy expenditure of being out there and being touched and dealing with everything.

'I wish the NFL could space out the London games because when they are on consecutive Sundays it's a grind for me. I crawl over the finish line. I've come to a point with the rising cost of living where I may no longer go to the dance any more. But I will continue to travel to London if I can afford the train tickets even if it's just so I can go to the free events to get the autographs for people.'

Sharing has been ingrained in Claire from a very young age and is at the heart of her NFL fandom. Her mother grew up an orphan and had an acute appreciation of anything that was shared with her. Claire knew she was in a privileged position and wanted other people to feel good too. 'There was a time when I was young where I had struggled with a question on a maths test. It was something like: "If you have 14 apples and you give eight to Jimmy, how many apples have you got left?" It didn't make sense to me. Why would you not give them all away? If I just keep hold of all this fruit it's going to rot and other people don't get to enjoy it.

'When I first did the giveaways I would save up money to buy a few things and then give them away to winners. I'm basically a happiness addict; I like making other people happy. My mum says I'm a giant Labrador in a person suit. I want you to be happy, but I don't need to be the person who makes you happy. I'll simply get happy off of your happiness and knowing I can be of service. I belong to some Facebook groups where you pay £5 and the money is pooled to buy something like a signed jersey or mini helmet. That was very useful for acquiring some special items in the early days of the giveaways. Then I started going to events that NFL UK would put on and get things signed.

'One time a guy called Francis got in touch with me to say he ran a small independent NFL shop down Exeter way. He said he'd seen my giveaways on social media and that he and the missus loved what I was doing. He told me they were going to shut down the shop because they were ready to retire and he wanted to send me some stuff for future giveaways. A few months later I was preparing for surgery and sat around with my friend Katherine. Francis ended up sending me an Excel spreadsheet of what stock they had. Katherine and I went through the list, colouring the things that I would like to get. At that point it could've just been ten key rings and I would've been happy because that would be ten key rings I didn't have to find myself. Lots of people with good intentions say they will send me stuff for giveaways but it never happens. I have learned over the years that just because I say something and stick to my word doesn't mean someone else is going to do that. A couple of months went by and I had heard nothing back. I thought that maybe he had sold the company wholesale. I couldn't really complain, they were his assets after all.'

This situation was very different. Francis came through big time for Claire. But really he came through for the entire NFL UK community whether they realised it or not. 'I went in to have surgery on my stomach and got that dealt with,' says Claire. 'I got home from the hospital and he sent me everything I requested from the list. It arrived at my place in like eight boxes, the sort of massive boxes you use to move house. Because of my surgery I wasn't even allowed to lift anything that weighed more than a kilo. I couldn't even put a pair of jeans on by myself at the time! I was not allowed to touch the boxes so I was lucky to have friends who could help get these boxes through my home and help me get them all open.

'It took two weeks to count and catalogue everything he had sent me. The stuff was everywhere. It wasn't in the bathroom or in my oven but other than that it was everywhere. Francis thanked me for taking it and his one stipulation was that I wasn't allowed to make any money off it which was fine by me. He said I could trade stuff with other people or sell some things as long as I didn't charge the retail price and that the money generated was turned into more giveaway swag for the community. This happened quite a while ago but it's been an approach I've stuck with because it's allowed me to create more giveaways. This delivery was the grandfather of NFL giveaways and I cannot thank Francis enough.'

One of the most popular – and oversubscribed – elements of an NFL weekend in London used to be the so-called tailgate parties staged outside Wembley Stadium. These were ticketed events when you could buy drinks, food and merchandise while soaking up the atmosphere with other fans. 'There was a VIP tailgate ticket raffle and luckily, I got in with my friend,' says Claire. 'She spotted a guy walking around wearing a Super Bowl ring. I've got a Super Bowl ring of my own. Mine is obviously a mock-up, so I said to this guy: "Is that a mock-up? It is so good. Please tell a girl where she can get that sort of level of mock-up! Or if it's real, I do apologise! I don't know who you are. Who are you?" And he replied: "I'm Tom Brady's dad." As you may have realised from the first thing I said to him, my mouth engages before my head does, so I blurted out: "Shut up and prove it." After all, anyone can say that, right? The fact that the man is wearing that ring proves nothing.'

Most people will have stories of how their mouth has got them in trouble at least once. Or maybe helped pave the way to a thrilling experience. Luckily for Claire it was the latter. 'He got out his wallet and showed me his ID,' she says. 'This really was Tom Brady's dad. This was when Tom had just three Super Bowl rings. We had a lovely chat, and he bought a drink for me and my friend. I talked to Tom's mom and told her that watching her son play football is like watching Picasso paint or watching the Bolshoi Ballet. I said: "We're watching someone at the pinnacle of excellence and I want you to know that I appreciate that." She told me that not only is it wonderful to hear from a female fan in another country who clearly knows what she's talking about, but that I wasn't saying it as a brown-nosing New England Patriots fan. She told me that as a mother she just wants to hear that her son is doing a good job. That genuinely touched me.'

There was something else Claire wanted to be touching too. Something she has developed a bit of a reputation for. 'I said to Tom Brady Sr that we were going to the game – after all, you can't get into the tailgate without tickets to the game. I pointed to the Super Bowl ring he was wearing and said: "Can I touch it? Can I put that on?" Before he could answer I told him he could hold my wallet. That way if the crazy urge to run away with the ring hit me he had some way of tracking me. I didn't think it would come to that but I hoped it would help persuade him. I explained he would find me instantly with the information in my wallet. Not to mention that I would struggle to get home with the ring because my train ticket was in there. He said: "OK, because you offered up the wallet we have a deal." So I got to wear a legit Super Bowl ring. I just thought: "Oh my gosh, this is amazing." And because of this experience when I now see a player wearing a Super Bowl ring I can't help myself, I have to ask if I can put it on. There are a few who say no, which is fine and totally understandable. But more often than not they say yes. I have been quite lucky. Eight Super Bowl rings and two Hall of Fame inductees so far.'

Claire's prominence in the scene and willingness to attend events has allowed her to witness some special moments in person. One of these times was when the Baltimore Ravens faced the Jacksonville Jaguars at Wembley in 2017. The game itself was a blowout, with the Ravens getting hammered 44-7 but there was still one high point on that trip at the Landmark Hotel in the Marylebone area of London. The hotel has become well known among UK fans as a base for NFL bigwigs ever since the International Series began. This is due to its proximity to Marylebone station, which offers a ten-minute direct train to Wembley Stadium station – a way to get to games without the fuss and crowds of the Tube network.

'I heard about an event at the Landmark Hotel and I knew I had to go,' says Claire. 'We've been lucky in the UK with the number of events the NFL will put on for fans. This one was almost like a religious experience. These NFL UK events are usually for audiences of between 200 and 500 fans. Sometimes they do smaller ones – these are intimate but not super intimate. This one was the opposite because the main guest was Ray Lewis. So many people wanted to meet him they had to open up the hotel's ballroom as well. There were more than 2,000 fans there. It was standing room only and there was a real buzz of excitement. When he walked in you could hear a pin drop. It was such a special experience and made you realise how privileged we are that the NFL will bring over a player of his calibre. They could do this for any country they want but they chose the UK. When Ray Lewis was speaking in that room, everyone – no matter what age, race, religion, or NFL team you followed – was hanging on that man's every word.'

The same game afforded Claire another Super Bowl ring opportunity, although this time it was a rare double dose of iconic jewellery. Claire was chosen to be involved in an activity ahead of the game which had her mixing in some interesting new circles. 'I was with my friend and we spotted two very well-dressed people in the area where we all had to meet up but these two were having a problem,' says Claire. 'They were struggling to put their lanyards together. I thought: "These people must be seriously well off if they can't do a simple task like that." So being the nice people we are, we went over to offer some help. I noticed their lanyards had an extra bit on – a special metal VIP thing. It looked very nice. Then I noticed something else. They were wearing Super Bowl rings! It turned out they were related to [one-time Ravens majority owner] Art Modell. Feeling cheeky, I just had to ask if I could get a picture of me wearing two different Ravens Super Bowl rings. So that's why there are pictures of me online with a Super Bowl XXXV ring and a Super Bowl XLVII ring.'

Not every fan in the UK is going to reach the extremes that Claire manages, and that's fine. She doesn't see herself as the ultimate fan, just one who wants to help others in the UK and give a good impression. This is where she sets a minimum standard for those who watch the sport. 'As much as I'm a big Bears fan, I also need to be bipartisan,' she says. 'Everyone has to be represented. I'll make some cheeky jokes or play up the panto behaviour on social media or out in public but it's all part of the fun.

'What I'm very much aware of is that I might be someone's first interaction with the NFL. I've got to behave in a way that is enticing, positive and inclusive. I want all fans in the UK to genuinely pause and think about this. Every time you put on your favourite team's jersey, T-shirt, hat or whatever, you are not only representing yourself, you are representing the league and your team. The NFL shield is on pretty much every piece of merchandise you can wear so you are representing that shield. Are you doing the best job you can when you do that? Are you warm? Are you welcoming? Are you behaving in a way that would make an eight-year-old child and an eighty-year-old grandmother want to interact with you? If the answer is no, please think about not wearing your NFL clothing in public.

'I've been to soccer matches in the UK where I haven't felt safe as a woman or as a disabled adult. That is not right. The internet is obviously not always the best place for a woman either. I'm a Bears fan but I don't care if you're a Packers fan, as long as you're warm and inclusive. I just want you to hold your hand out and invite others to this party, because we're having a great time. I had a negative interaction with a fan of a particular Scottish football team on a train and it has put me off Scottish football. That was one interaction with one person. An NFL fan in the UK could put a potential fan off the sport. So please think about your behaviour. If you can't handle your alcohol, stop drinking. If you can't handle that your team will lose, stop being a sports fan because losing is part of the game. If you can't be polite, if you can't be respectful about your opponent, just get out, go be toxic somewhere else – not in my playground. Everyone has the potential to be a superfan and everyone should take that opportunity if that's what they want to do. Just remember, that like a superhero, with great power comes great responsibility. For superfans, with great visibility comes great responsibility.'

There are few fans in the UK who are greater advocates for the sport than Claire. She's been a fan as far back as she can remember and shows no sign of stopping. 'I can't stand it when people in this country say American football is boring and that it goes on for four hours but nothing happens,' she says. 'What?! When I go to a game I pay for my seat but I only use the three inches nearest the edge for most of it. I guess not only have I drunk the NFL Kool Aid, I'm administering Kool Aid to other people. I'm practically force-feeding them.'

The British discover tailgating

'MY GIRLFRIEND was from a culture where you don't just wait for the other person to go off for 17 weeks, so my plan didn't go down very well,' says Adam Goldstein, known to many as the Tailgate Knight.

Adam had broken the news to his girlfriend that he was going to relocate to the US for the duration of the 2008 NFL season so he could immerse himself in local fan culture. To fund the adventure he had to sell his home. 'My girlfriend's ex was a big Watford FC fan and she had seen for herself the sexism within British soccer culture,' says Adam. 'She didn't like that. She said to me: "You're not laddish. You like theatre and drama. I don't get it!" She didn't really understand what the NFL could be like. It's why I wanted to bring her out to America while I was there. I wasn't saying she should attend 30 games in a year. That's a lot. But I thought if she came to a few games and ate some barbecue it would be fun.'

Not many people do what Adam did in 2008 but plenty of people did what he did in the mid-1980s. He started watching the NFL on Channel 4 and became hooked on the Chicago Bears because of Super Bowl XX. 'It was a great time,' says Adam. 'I loved it all. I loved watching it and I loved buying stickers for the [Panini] sticker albums and of course collecting the bubblegum helmets [made by Leaf].'

Like many young Brits, Adam was surrounded by soccer fans and had first-hand experience of it himself. 'My dad was always a big Tottenham Hotspur fan but as a kid, when

I compared the two sports, I clearly preferred American football. It looked brash, colourful and fun. As I got older and went through secondary school, it kind of set me apart. People were like: "Oh, Goldstein's the guy into American football." And that meant I got even more into it because I wasn't part of the norm. I got teased because of it sometimes. I was told it was rugby with pads or whatever but I stuck with it.

'In the early days of Channel 4 I knew what a touchdown was but I didn't know what the four downs were about until my dad explained it. I think my dad eventually got into it because I was into it. He would get the salt and pepper pots and showed me how teams lined up. I used to go to soccer matches at Leyton Orient back then. I remember thinking it was a drag, not helped by me witnessing a riot there. There were no cheerleaders. No colour. No razzmatazz. Americana was so enticing in the 1980s. It could be *Dynasty* or it could be the Dallas Cowboys, it was simply very appealing.'

The sport seemed exotic to Adam and other young fans in the UK. Something that seemed very distant. 'It didn't ever occur to me that someone like me would either play or coach the sport in any organised way,' he says. 'With soccer I knew anyone could play. I felt that the NFL was a million miles away. It seemed gladiatorial and an exclusive sport for superstar athletes. I did well enough academically to be offered a scholarship to a really posh boys' school. The only sports to play there were rugby union, soccer and cricket. I most enjoyed playing rugby because it was the closest to American football.

'When I was 13 we were told that we all had to do an individual five-minute talk on a subject we liked outside of academia. I picked American football because I wanted to talk to them about something they didn't already know much about. Luckily I knew all about the four down rule and beyond by that point. After I gave the talk I got a round of applause and this cemented the fact that it was OK to love a sport that wasn't soccer. At that point I got more and more into it.'

Teenaged Adam was reading *First Down* each week and finding that his love for the sport was creeping into all areas of his life. 'When I had my bar mitzvah, I had an American football theme,' he says. 'Every table was named after a different NFL team, with the Bears as the top table of course. The colours for the event had a navy and orange theme. Even now as an adult I always wear a piece of orange clothing. What I was unaware of at the time was the fact there was a flag football team very close to my home. I only found out about it many years later. My parents weren't to know – it wasn't something you could just easily look up back then.

'The closest I got to playing the sport as a kid was through the *John Madden Football* games. Although the game itself was fun I used it more like Wikipedia. I could turn it on and find every NFL wide receiver, for example. It was a great way to learn about all the players. At this point in my life everyone in my family knew that if they were getting me a present for my birthday or Christmas it was probably going to be a book on American football which fed my obsession even more. I've still got those books because I never throw anything away that is connected to the NFL.

'My family discovered a shop in Dagenham that sold lots of American sports stuff so they'd often get me things from there. Proper NFL merchandise felt like a very exclusive thing back then. Everything is more accessible now, to the point where just today I gave a player I coach a Deion Sanders bobblehead. I wanted to wear NFL clothing to send a message about my interests. I always had a chip on my shoulder about it. I probably put myself in the firing line with my choices because it made it clear: "I don't really want to watch rugby, I don't really like football, I like this other thing." People thought I was a bit kooky but I stuck to my guns.'

Although the sport felt very distant in his youth, Adam feels that part of the reason the NFL has become so big in the UK is that fans have been able to experience the product in the flesh. For those who have been lucky enough to have seen a game in the US the experience is much stronger because of everything that happens around it. 'There are different reasons for going to an NFL game or attending any cultural event,' says Adam. 'You'll have the fans going to a concert saying: "Oh my God, the band's gonna play this or that." But sometimes it's just a catalyst to help you have a good time and the concert, the movie or the NFL game itself are probably a bit of a side story.

'I went to see The Rolling Stones at Hyde Park in London. Personally, I'm more into drum and bass, but one of my best friends flew over to the UK having bought a pair of tickets and wanted me to come with him. To be honest, we had a good time all day. It was like tailgating in a way. My friend wasn't as into it as I thought he would be considering he'd paid £100 for the tickets. For him it was just a way for us to go out and have a great day. It wasn't totally about the music, just like going to an NFL game isn't totally about the sport. I used to go out to the theatre quite a lot and part of the attraction was having a ticket to get out of the house and do something.'

The sports of American football and British soccer have some similarities but the experience of going to a game is markedly different. 'Tailgating is obviously a significant part of the NFL gameday experience,' says Adam. 'Soccer in the UK doesn't have that. If you're a soccer fan you may go to watch the game and that's it. But there are lots of soccer fans who are also into the whole culture around the sport. When I was growing up that simply meant going to the pub and drinking a lot before and after the match. When I went to soccer matches as a little boy with my dad I saw hooliganism and riots. Even then I thought it was bizarre and I didn't feel safe at all. The first American football game I ever went to was a preseason American Bowl at Wembley in 1990 when the Los Angeles Raiders played the New Orleans Saints. Before the game I thought: "Oh my God, who should we support?" We went with the Saints but ended up sitting among Raiders fans. I thought at the time we'd be in trouble but of course everything was totally fine. No one was trying to start a fight. Looking back, I think I was being harsh on soccer at the time but it genuinely felt to me like the sport was simply about having a fight and getting drunk. People might drink a lot during a tailgate party but it's very different to the drinking culture of soccer.'

Sure, some people – a very small minority – will go to a tailgate to get wasted. But the point of tailgating isn't to get hammered, it's to socialise, meet fans of your team and your opponent, and outdo one another with your grilling skills. 'I remember going to Cleveland and the New York Giants were coming to town as the defending Super Bowl champions,' says Adam. 'I met Browns fans who were excited because the Giants were a big market team and it was *Monday Night Football*. For me, as an NFL fan in the UK, all the teams in the league are big. They all have stadiums bigger than 60,000 [only four Premier League soccer teams have stadiums of this size].

'Locals told me it was good because travelling Giants fans would ensure a sell-out. I couldn't understand why they'd want rival fans buying lots of tickets! In soccer you don't want that because the away fans would come in, be loud and take away your home advantage. I asked: "Why do you want all their fans to be in the stadium making noise on third down?" They told me it was better for the stadium and the city. Browns fans were happy that the hotels would be full because the city would make a lot of money from local taxes. Many new stadiums in the NFL are funded, at least in part, by hotel taxes, the idea being the local people don't pay for the new stadium – out-of-town visitors to the stadium do.

'It sounds like a *Freakonomics* essay but it's a big deal. Cleveland as a city really welcomed Giants fans and so did the Browns fans who tailgated. Meanwhile, if a soccer fan from London goes to a match in the north of England and decides to stay overnight in a hotel – most won't – that tax money doesn't stay local. It just goes in one big national pot. Because of the way it works in America all fans are welcome and it means a more inclusive atmosphere. I think this is in part because a team can go eight years without playing a road game against a particular team. In UK soccer you know you're guaranteed to play every team in your league home and away every single season.'

The welcome that awaits visiting fans to NFL cities is powerful and for anyone used to the soccer landscape in the UK, it's quite an eye-opener. 'Before West Ham moved to the Olympic Stadium and were in their traditional home at Upton Park, people would board up their houses on a matchday if they lived near the stadium,' says Adam. 'I used to wonder why people would choose to live near a sports stadium. But when I went to Green Bay, I saw a four- or five-mile stretch towards Lambeau Field lined with Packers-themed houses. You know you are entering Packers territory but that doesn't mean they aren't welcoming. In general America is a very welcoming place, especially if you have a British accent.'

The point where Adam discovered his favourite part of the NFL gameday experience was at a legendary *Monday Night Football* in Arizona. That night, the Bears were not who Adam thought they were, so he walked out and had a life-changing experience. 'In 2006 my friend was getting married in LA,' says Adam, 'and a buddy of mine suggested extending the holiday. He said we could hop on a plane headed to Arizona and go to see a *Monday Night Football* game between the Cardinals and the Bears. Of course I thought this was a good idea even though my friend wasn't a huge fan of the sport. Like British people with no understanding of tailgating we got to the stadium about ten minutes before kick-off. And I ended up walking out late in the third quarter because the Bears were losing by 20 points. Obviously I had no idea that Devin Hester and Brian Urlacher were going to help the Bears win with an incredible comeback.

'As we got out of the stadium we heard a huge roar and knew it must've been a touchdown. That's when I started to spot a lot of people in the car park gathered around TVs. I couldn't believe they were so close to the stadium but watching it outside on a screen. We then watched the rest of the game on someone's TV, who had a satellite dish powered by a generator and was also cooking up hot dogs. The Bears of course won at the death and I thought: "We need to get out of here now or we're gonna get stabbed." But as we went to leave, the guy whose TV we had been watching said we had to stay for hot dogs.

"It's *Monday Night Football*," he told us. "We have to celebrate. We haven't had *Monday Night Football* here since the 1990s." I said: "Yeah, but I'm not one of you. I'm not a Cardinals fan." He replied: "So what?" We stayed there for about another hour just talking and eating hot dogs. That's when it kicked in how weird this seemed to someone used to sport in the UK. How was it you're allowed to barbecue outside a stadium? How's he got a TV? How were there so many people doing the exact same thing? At that point I had the bright idea to spend a week in each city that was hosting *Monday Night Football* to see what it meant to each community or its team. That idea evolved into something else.'

That something else turned into one of the most famous road trips any UK fan has done in honour of the NFL. It caused him to sell his home and walk out on his girlfriend – so it had better be a pretty enticing trip. 'I started to think that I would have a target of going to 17 primetime games so I could compare them,' says Adam, 'but the more I thought about it the more I felt it wasn't a fair test. I wouldn't see every team and I'd be in some cities multiple times. Plus, a night game feels different to a day game. It's one thing setting up a tailgate in the late afternoon, it's another getting up at the crack of dawn to do it for a noon kick-off. I also wanted to make sure I saw the whole spectrum from big, hot cities to cold, small places, such as Green Bay. I wanted to really get inside the world of tailgating and figure out the different ways people tailgate in different locations, because the likes of Channel 4 and Sky had never devoted much time to it despite it being part of the fabric of the NFL. Tailgating culture is such a big deal but the typical fan in the UK didn't know anything about it at the time. I actually felt annoyed with myself for having so little knowledge about it.'

Adam decided this was a trip he needed to do. Not just because he enjoyed tailgating in Arizona but because of the way he felt about the sport when he was younger. 'Like I say, I had a chip on my shoulder about the fact I was an NFL fan and some people didn't take the sport seriously in the UK,' says Adam. 'One of the reasons I did the trip was to push that chip on my shoulder away. In 2000, I was living in Toronto

and a friend of mine suggested we go to Buffalo to catch a
Bills game when Doug Flutie was their quarterback. We got
on a coach and it took six hours to get there. That's me as a
Bears fan travelling all that way and it's not even my team
playing. I did it because going to an NFL game is a fun day
out no matter who is playing. I recently went on a stag do
in Newcastle, and no one in the group – not even the soccer
fans – were suggesting we go to a Newcastle United soccer
match because none of us supported that team or who they
were playing. Why would we bother? An NFL game would
be different, in part because of everything around it, such
as the food and the camaraderie. So my plan was to travel
around and write a blog about my experiences.'

All he had to do to make it work was to sell his home
and tell his girlfriend he was leaving the country. 'I kind of
had the idea in my head before I met her,' Adam says. 'I told
myself not to worry and that it would work out. I took the
chunk of money from selling the flat and told my girlfriend
I'd be back in 17 weeks and that it would be great if she flew
out to experience some of it with me. Obviously she was
sceptical about the whole thing.'

Adam wanted to back the home team at each game he
went to. The plan went out the window almost immediately.
'The first primetime Sunday night game of the season was
in Indianapolis,' says Adam. 'The Bears were the road team
against the Colts so the experiment wasn't going to work
that day! Travelling around I never had an issue with the
fact I was a Bears fan. And nobody cared that I was a fan of
one team but that I was choosing to be a fan of another team
that day. Can you imagine that in the UK? A Tottenham fan
going to an Arsenal match and supporting them that day? I
think the typical American view was that I was a fan of the
sport. They knew I must've put a lot of money into the trip

and had left my job to do something that, although it was admittedly a self-indulgent and fun trip, was also something that would hopefully publicise the NFL in a positive way and give tailgating some international attention.'

The plan to cover his adventure in a blog seemed like the best course of action so Adam followed that for a while. That was until he realised he could take the story to another level. 'I was writing the blog and it eventually occurred to me that it could be a book,' he says. 'I wrote a skeleton of the book, which ended up being the opening chapter, and I sent it off to agents and publishers. I didn't get anywhere. No one was interested. Meanwhile, somebody got in touch with me to say they were going to run a trip in the 2009 season. The plan was for it to be sponsored by Cholula hot sauce and they would go to games and hit the tailgate parties. They wanted me to come along as the tailgate expert and live on a school bus which would be driven from game to game. It was great to be a tailgater and cook for hundreds of people. Midway through that trip I heard from someone who worked at a very small publisher called Potomac saying they wanted me to write the book for them. I went back to my parents' home having sold my flat and got to work.'

If Adam thought he could simply funnel his blog into a Word document and be done with it he would be mistaken. 'I took the blog, which was big, and turned it into a manuscript that had way too many words,' he says. 'When I was getting rejections, I heard a few times that the publisher didn't want to hear about my journey. They felt that wasn't very interesting. They said there should be more about tailgating, which isn't what I expected. I had not read a lot of non-fiction, certainly not a lot of sports books. Maybe *Friday Night Lights*, and one or two others – that was it. So I panicked a bit and decided to dig deep into a lot of American football books and general sports books. I had to figure out how I could say something different.

'The first draft I sent to Potomac was about America's relationship with TV through the NFL based on my experience on the first trip. There was a chapter on tailgating, a chapter on travel, and so on. It was much more academic than the blog because I had done so much reading. Potomac got back to me saying: "Yeah, this is great but it's really academic." They wanted it massively simplified with a structure that followed the format of Game One, then Game Two etc. They wanted a full rewrite in just two weeks. At this point I was directing a play at the Edinburgh Festival Fringe so I had no idea how I could get it done. Luckily for me the 2011 NFL lockout happened. Potomac was worried the book would be released while the players were on strike and games would be cancelled. This gave me some breathing room because the release was put back to 2012. I had time to do the rewrite and what you see in the book now is basically what I turned in.'

The book, which had forewords from Sky Sports NFL host Neil Reynolds and tailgate legend Karen DiEugenio (she and her husband used to spend their lives driving around the US tailgating, home-schooling their kids along the way), was received warmly by fans on both sides of the Atlantic. For many UK fans, eager to read about Adam's adventure, it was their first real insight into the world of tailgating. 'A lot of people loved it, which was a relief because I didn't know who I was writing for at the time,' says Adam. 'As far as the American publisher was concerned, I was writing it for a US audience – the story of this wacky Brit shining a light on their sport. In the end, it sold better in the UK and it helped more British people get into tailgating.

'But the use of the word in the UK has changed now. NFL UK has done a pretty good job of making the word mean "a party for fans" with their "tailgate" fan zones at games in London, which don't actually have any tailgating. But it can be hard to explain the appeal of tailgating to the UK fans. If you just boil it down to having some beers and barbecue, I think British people will go: "Is that it? Like they do at the Green Man pub near Wembley Stadium? We've done it." But that really isn't a tailgate. When I was writing the book, it was more to show British people the deep appeal of tailgating and try to explain the culture of it. It's great that the NFL comes to Twickenham, Wembley and Tottenham. The International Series is fun and you get a good sense of the game. You don't get the real NFL experience, though. More UK fans are going to games in the US now and many are going to the tailgates. About 15 to 20 times a year I link UK fans with particular tailgaters in the US so they know where to go and who to see.'

Tailgate to Heaven was followed by *The Tailgate Knight Rises*, a book about his trip on the modified school bus. By this time Adam had become well known within the US tailgate community and he always felt like he was representing his country when he was meeting American fans. 'They were genuinely appreciative that their sport was going international,' says Adam. 'Most fans in the US are now fully aware that the NFL has gone global but back in 2008 they were surprised and kept telling me how cool it was that people from abroad were into it. They asked me a lot of questions about the American football coverage in the UK and wanted to know how I came to be an NFL fan. They were fascinated by the fact I'd played the sport competitively at my university for a year as well. Because it's a niche sport in the UK, it's more accommodating in a lot of ways.

'In the US, you can play if you're good enough. If you don't make it into your high school team, or you do but then aren't recruited to play at the college level, then maybe – just maybe – you will play flag football with your buddies. But probably not, because it's a pain setting up a team or a league. In British culture, American football, from a participation point of view, is a community sport. If you are prepared to pay for your equipment then you'll be in a team. It's not considered to be for the elite athletes, it's just for fun. That's how a skinny ten-stone student like me ended up playing cornerback at university.'

As much as the fans Adam met on his travels wanted to learn about what UK fans were like, they also wanted to compare themselves with domestic rivals. The world of NFL tailgating was more competitive than Adam expected, although not strictly in the ways people might imagine. 'Fans of each team really wanted me to spread a message about them and tell their story,' says Adam. 'Fans would say things like: "Make sure you tell everyone that our team has the nicest fans," or perhaps the best beer or most delicious food. It mattered what other people thought of them and their tailgates. I was told by one set of fans, "When you go to the Saints, you tell them that we have the best food." Not the best players or the best draft picks. It was all about "We have the best food and we are the nicest fans." Everyone wanted to compete to be the nicest fans! Not the most modest fans! I think this has something to do with how welcoming Americans can be to outsiders.

'There was also a bit of unexpected prejudice however. Some people looked at the schedule on the back of the T-shirt I had made and said things like: "Oh my God, you're going to Oakland?" I was like: "Should I not?" And do you know what? Oakland was great. I've been there three times now and it's been awesome every time. If I see genuinely drunk and disorderly people at any game anywhere I stay away from them. The fans I met in Oakland were among the most appreciative that I'd made the trip. They thanked me for coming to their city and stadium. Fans in Oakland used to get a bad rap, and the same applies to fans in Buffalo to a certain extent.'

Adam's schooldays are well behind him and he's had various NFL adventures in his adult life. Nowadays you're more likely to find him on the sidelines than you are on a sofa watching games. 'I spend a lot of time coaching,' says Adam. 'There are under-16 and under-19 teams, plus a women's team. I don't watch the NFL quite as much as I used to and I'm not as obsessive about the Chicago Bears as I used to be. I can't tell you who's the current starting left tackle, for instance, but I could've told you the answer 15 years ago. I think that's because once I started coaching I devoted more time to that. I have a teaching background and I want to use my enthusiasm to help young people to get into the sport in the way that I didn't.

'I didn't know about the Xs and Os back then. It's obviously such an interesting sport from a tactical point of view and no one really ever told me that when I was young. Now I spend a lot of time working on whiteboards in the kitchen. If you walked into my house you'd spot me figuring out what to do about next week's opponents. I have all these schematics and then have to figure out what will work when you're dealing with 15-year-old kids. I'm probably over-egging the pudding. You know they just want to take the ball and run as fast as they can. I've possibly moved slightly away from the NFL and more into coaching purely because I can control the coaching. As a coach I've been genuinely impressed by the amount of understanding my players have. They know their stuff. Because the NFL is so mainstream in the US there is a greater percentage of casual fans. Over

THE AMERICAN FOOTBALL REVOLUTION

here, because it's relatively niche, if you're into it, you have to be a lot more into it than the typical fan in America. Even the knowledge of tailgating has shot up in the UK. Maybe my books have helped.'

Adam's massive road trips may be in the rear-view mirror but certain things haven't changed that much. Wondering what happened to the girlfriend Adam left behind to tour the NFL's tailgates? She married him. 'We had a navy and orange-themed wedding,' says Adam.

Tapping into a British love of betting

AT THE end of a *Thursday Night Football* game in 2022, the Cleveland Browns scored a defensive touchdown against the Pittsburgh Steelers on the final play to win the game 29-17 rather than 23-17. Prime Video announcer Al Michaels said: 'That may be meaningful for some of you and you know who I mean.' It was a moment that showed how acceptable sports betting now was to the establishment. The broadcast crew, just like the people in the NFL's head office, knew that there were plenty of people watching the game purely because they had bet money on it.

Betting on sport is woven into the fabric of British fandom. Despite efforts from various governments to control or lessen the influence of gambling, the pursuit has been popular for centuries. From the 1960s onwards it was easy for any fan to walk into a bookmakers in any UK high street and place bets on various sports. Although horse racing had always been the primary focus, the opening of these betting shops allowed a wider number of sports, especially team sports, to be bet on.

Regulation in the US has been far stricter and required a potential sports gambler to have access to either a casino or a semi-legal bookmaker. It wasn't until the ubiquity of the internet that there were simple ways to place bets as a US citizen – providing you knew the legal workarounds.

The online gambling explosion was different in the UK and meant that all sports bettors had a level of freedom and flexibility they could never have imagined before. The rise of satellite and cable sports coverage also meant they could watch and bet on sports leagues that would have previously been a mystery. Plus, the number of matches being shown meant that people would bet on more than just the winner. Want to bet on how many corners there will be in a particular soccer match? Go ahead, then watch the match yourself for the excitement. Through the first two decades of the 21st century, UK online bookmakers also devoted a lot of space to the NFL, despite its status as a niche sport.

Ollie Thornton, a producer and broadcaster who co-hosts the Edge Rush NFL betting podcast, says that timings on a Sunday in the UK helped turn American football into a staple for those who enjoy a flutter. 'I was a university student when I first started watching *NFL RedZone*,' he says. 'I'd wake up at midday, probably watch the lunchtime Premier League match on Sky Sports, then the 4pm kick-off. It was perfect because you'd have those two matches and then about ten minutes later the NFL games would kick off on Sky. You're hungover, so what else are you going to do? You're not gonna get off the sofa because you're a student and it's Sunday. You might go to lectures tomorrow, but who knows? So those Premier League matches would flow straight into the NFL.'

However, Ollie's journey into NFL fandom didn't start with betting, it started with another institution that played a formative role in the lives of many UK fans: NFL Films. 'My first memory of American football is the 2009 season of *Hard Knocks* on the Cincinnati Bengals. It was on at about 11am on Channel 4 with links by [UK TV personality and avid NFL fan] Vernon Kay. It must've been edited because I don't remember any explicit language. I do remember thinking: "What is this?" At that point, I was obsessed with sport, especially football, cricket and rugby union because those were sports I played. This was also the first exposure I ever had to a fly-on-the-wall sports documentary and I found it absolutely fascinating. I became obsessed with Chad Ochocinco, finding him incredibly entertaining. I thought Carson Palmer was really cool at the time. I loved everything about quarterbacks. And then watching the players getting cut and essentially seeing what goes on behind the scenes at a sports organisation – for a kid who was obsessed with watching sport and live games – was huge.

Hard Knocks has not only played a big part in getting UK fans up to speed with what goes on at an NFL franchise, it's also created its own small industry. This in turn feeds into the demands of an international audience. You just need to look at how many other sports and countries have followed the massively successful *Hard Knocks* format. 'Hard Knocks was a pioneer for what came after,' says Ollie. 'There are similar documentaries about other teams. Many are doing it in-house – the Jets, the Browns, they all do YouTube series that are essentially their own-brand versions of *Hard Knocks*. This in turn led to *All Or Nothing*, which follows teams through the season rather than ahead of the season. There are so many of them going on: there's a Crystal Palace FC version and a radio documentary series covering Rotherham United FC's season.'

Ollie, being a sports buff, also gives credit to what came before. 'Arguably the grandfather of these sports documentaries – which you probably couldn't show now because of how dated they are – were for the British and Irish Lions rugby union tours against southern hemisphere teams,' says Ollie. 'That first *Living With Lions*, made during the 1997 tour of South Africa, is so old school that I'm pretty sure half the things they say would see modern players cancelled if they repeated them, but it reflected the majority of rugby union players at the time.'

For a young sports-mad kid with no idea what the NFL was, *Hard Knocks* was a hell of a drug. 'The first time I saw it I simply stumbled across it on a Sunday morning. These were the days before you could choose to watch whatever you wanted whenever you wanted. I was probably just waiting for [young adult-focused soap opera] *Hollyoaks* to come on. But the thing is, even though I was enthralled by it, I wasn't surrounded by anyone else who loved the sport. I had no other way to engage with it. I had no idea when the next episode was going to be released. I had no concept of what the season looked like or when it was going to start.'

Things changed for Ollie when his family got Sky TV, opening up a world of live sport. 'That happened in about 2011 or 2012,' he says, 'and I finally started following the NFL a bit, although I didn't start watching it regularly until I went to university. I tried to make a point of watching *Hard Knocks* episodes every week once we had Sky Sports. I remember there was a point where they broadcast a load of them overnight. I always struggled to sleep as a kid so I just stayed up and watched about three or four in a row. That was when I became a Cincinnati Bengals fan because they were the only team I really knew of.

'I realised that the sport was pretty cool, but at the same time didn't really understand the rules, or what the sport actually was. I certainly didn't know how much I would grow to like it. None of my family or friends at the time had any interest in American football. They were often quite dismissive. In the case of my dad, he is incredibly dismissive of American sports. His assessment of NBA basketball is that there is too much squeaking.

'He buys into that very cliched British viewpoint that the NFL is too "stop-start" and that they only play for seven minutes. He believes that it's all a waste of time. It was hard for me to really watch anything of the NFL at that point because he'd be in control of the TV most Sundays. And my sister and my mum certainly weren't going to sit and watch the NFL with me on another TV. So I was deprived of that for a very long period of time. Other than *Hard Knocks* I'd only end up watching the Super Bowls because I knew when they were going to be on and they had a lot of coverage in the UK building up to it. Super Bowl XLVIII between the Seattle Seahawks and Denver Broncos was the first one where I sat down to watch the whole thing. I was incredibly disappointed because it was a blowout.'

And it was the following Super Bowl that inspired Ollie to place his first bet. He put money on the Seahawks to beat the New England Patriots. Unfortunately for Ollie, two late touchdowns from the Patriots, combined with a goal-line interception, cost the Seahawks the championship. 'I think that was the first moment where I realised how fun a sport American football is to gamble on,' says Ollie. 'I've since had situations where I've thought that I was guaranteed to lose, and I've ended up winning. And in that situation, where Seattle had the ball at the one-yard line, I had the opposite. I genuinely thought I was guaranteed to win the bet. It was ripped away from me in a moment where I didn't really understand how it happened. Everyone was saying to me it was over. That the Seahawks would run the ball and they were going to win.'

For Ollie, it wasn't about being up or down financially that night, it was about the extra dimension it gave an already layered sport. It was a way into a game that, to those who grow up outside North America, will often feel rather complicated and alien. 'I was a student at the time so the maximum I would've bet on a game was probably £10,' says Ollie. 'One of my friends had bet a lot more money than I had bet on the game, and also had the Seahawks to win. Watching his reaction after Malcolm Butler's interception was so entertaining that I got over losing my £10 pretty quickly. His reaction to the fact that they had lost in such a way was hilarious. I've never heard someone curse out Russell Wilson so much in my entire life. I don't think I've ever heard anyone curse out any player in that way since then either. After that moment I realised the emotion that it had created for me and for him. I personally found that really enticing.'

In the history of the modern NFL, there have probably been few higher-profile moments that could sell a sceptical audience on the appeal of American football than the Seahawks snatching defeat from the jaws of victory that night. And it was also the ideal advertisement for how exciting placing a bet could be for some fans. 'That play was the moment that set me up for the following season,' says Ollie. 'The next year, I was like: "OK, I really like this sport. Watching that Super Bowl was so much fun." It was a perfect example of how a game can go back and forth. It was a game where you never really knew who was going to win. It showed how incredible these athletes are. How clutch they are and how it is all dependent on how they perform in a critical moment. I love that about sports. I think that's what defines a sportsman or sportswoman: what they are able to do in that moment where it's all on the line.'

A new Sunday routine was set for Ollie and his friends: watching a couple of Premier League soccer matches and then at 6pm switching to the NFL. 'I genuinely think one of the biggest reasons why all my friends and I were into the NFL so much was because of the 6pm start right after the soccer,' says Ollie. 'If you are already drinking beers and eating unhealthy food, and you already love sport, why wouldn't you just carry on? It was so enticing. The NFL games had such great production values you would find yourself drawn in. There is, however, one thing that is always a potential deterrent to a British fan, and that is the stop-start nature of the sport. Most British sports are not built that way. So I can understand some new fans being put off by the fact that you can watch a bit at the start of a game and then it goes straight to an ad break. If a game starts with two three-and-out drives, that can immediately put you off from watching a full NFL game because you feel like you're watching more adverts than action. *NFL RedZone* was the perfect catalyst to allow us to sit there on the sofa and be constantly entertained. And then the perfect side note to that was an accumulator.'

An accumulator, for those who don't know, is one bet that combines multiple games into one single wager. The odds are multiplied so the potential payout is obviously larger, the downside being that if your accumulator had ten outcomes within it and you got nine correct, you win nothing. Sometimes an accumulator can include multiple sports at once. 'They work so well together,' says Ollie. 'It is ridiculous how much thought we put into it. Back then, we would put a couple of little bets on the 2pm and then the 4pm Premier League kick-offs, plus maybe some soccer matches in Europe just to boost the bet. As students, we didn't really have any money. So we would be putting £3 on and trying to win £100.'

As well as the potential payout, it gave Ollie, his friends, and many others across the UK, a reason to care – which is always important if it's a sport that isn't deep-rooted in local culture. 'It gave me a team to support every single day,' says Ollie. If the Bengals weren't playing in that window, then I would suddenly become a huge Kansas City Chiefs fan or I'd suddenly become a huge Raiders fan because that's who I had in my accumulator at the time.

'I would just be waiting for news via *NFL RedZone* in the same way that you're waiting for the moment on Sky Sports' *Soccer Saturday* when Jeff Stelling says something like: "And there's been a goal at Norwich!" You're waiting for that moment where they switch to the game you've bet on. Say, the Broncos are in the red zone or maybe there's been an insane play for the Raiders. There's that moment of excitement where you wonder if it's gone in your favour or gone against you. You never quite know until it's on the screen.

'The NFL is even better than soccer in this regard because there are so many more possibilities. When they say on *Soccer Saturday* there's been a goal, you know it's either going to be a goal for your team or a goal against your team. Whereas in the NFL a highlight could be one of many things. Maybe the team driving scores a touchdown, but there could easily be a pick six, or maybe a fumble recovery for a touchdown by the defense. There's no reason why you won't see a turnover. You have no idea what's about to happen. The possibilities are endless. Which in turn means there's endless entertainment. You're just always excited and enthralled by what's about to happen.'

In the famous *Simpsons* episode 'Lisa The Greek' (with its title being a reference to Jimmy 'The Greek' Snyder, who would subtly give tips to gamblers on the CBS pregame show *The NFL Today*), Homer and Lisa spend their Sundays watching NFL games, in part because Lisa is great at predicting winners. Homer says that as good as ice cream is, it's even better if you cover it with hot fudge, whipped cream and 'crumbled up cookie things'. This leads Lisa to conclude that 'Gambling makes a good thing even better'.

Obviously that's not the case for everyone. Betting is harmless fun for many. Some might feel that betting £10 during *NFL RedZone* while having a few beers and pizzas at home with friends is a better financial decision than watching in a sports bar and having to pay their prices for food and drink. However, for others, staying in control is impossible. The desire to chase losses becomes all-consuming. The pursuit of money will affect people in different ways, a key reason why governments through US history have regulated it so tightly.

'The money isn't what entices me,' says Ollie. 'What I love is the feeling that I know more than another person and that I've used my knowledge to beat the bookies. I find that really compelling. When I was a student I would probably put about £20 a month into my online betting account. I would usually put a quid or two on a big one that could win something like £100. Then I'd probably put £3 or £4 on bets that could win about £20. These would be a bit more sensible, the ones that I actually think are going to happen. And usually I was pretty good. This was one of the ways I made money at university aside from part-time jobs.'

Some gamblers will tell you they have a system. Ollie certainly did but it was more about using the bookies' desire to bring in new customers against them. 'The betting companies used to have offers where you would sign up and get £50 of free bets or something like that,' he says. 'So I said to my flatmate who looked after the household bills, give me your accounts. I'll bet in your accounts and then whatever I win goes towards the bills. So I didn't pay any bills during the last few years of university because I did so well gambling with free money on offer. This only works if you win but at the same time, when you're winning with free money, it's a lot easier.

'When people talk to me about gambling they say people always lose. That ultimately everyone is down. I think for the general masses, that is the case. It doesn't apply to me or others like me. I'm quite a stingy person. I'm not a huge gambler. I don't like casinos very much. They don't give me the same thrill as I get from betting on the NFL because I just feel like most of the time in a casino it's luck. I don't have any insight into the person opposite me. I can tell you statistics for blackjack, but that doesn't give me an edge over the dealer. With sports gambling, I feel like I have an edge over the bookie because of the amount that I watch the NFL and the amount that I know about it. I've spent time researching it because I love watching it.

'I've only ever bet quite low stakes and quite sensibly unless I win big. Then suddenly, if I win big, that money becomes really easy for me to lose. That's where gambling is bad. Your senses get skewed. It means that suddenly winning £20 doesn't give you the same kind of buzz any more and it needs to be a £300 win instead. I've done my best to get over that feeling because I'm self-aware enough to realise that any money is good money to win.'

Ollie's self-confessed stinginess has served him well. He points out that from the age of 18 it would've been legal for him to put his entire salary into an online gambling account each month, it's just that he chooses not to. 'All these sites give you the option of setting a daily limit for yourself,' he says. 'I don't bother with this because there's nothing stopping a user from setting that limit at 20 grand. And then straightaway putting all that money on a match in the Belgian soccer league's third division. And this is because it is so very easy to gamble.

'I probably have about a 55 per cent win rate. So I'm 5 per cent up from what my stake is, which is still up, even if it's not by that much. To be completely honest with you, even if I were down 5 per cent, I would still feel exactly the same way about it because of how much enjoyment I've got out of it.

Even when I've lost money betting on the NFL it's still been fun. I would have done even better if I didn't make stupid bets to win silly amounts of money. That's where you end up losing. I think if I had always been much more sensible I'd be a lot more up.'

With casual sports gambling being so ingrained in British culture it's no surprise that Ollie was exposed to it at a young age. 'I've been picking bets for the Grand National since I was four years old,' Ollie says. 'That's the most famous annual horse race in the UK and unlike, say, the NFL, it exists solely because of gambling. Horse racing is why betting shops used to be such a big deal over here, but they are the most miserable places in the world if you go inside them. It's no surprise that gambling became much more enticing once you could do it online. I enjoy betting on accumulators online and part of what's good about them is that you have to wait for those games to be played. It takes a few hours. You can't then immediately do another. It's not like another spin of the roulette wheel or the horse race that's happening straight after. It's a slate of games you're interested in and if you're betting on an NFL accumulator you'll wait a week for your next shot. It keeps you disciplined.'

Games of chance leave Ollie cold but the storylines and the many 'games within the games' make the NFL engrossing for him and others. 'You form an emotional attachment in the moment with high-level sport. There was a game a few seasons ago that means I will forever slightly despise the Seattle Seahawks. I had an accumulator riding into the late night game where they were favourites to win. I was insanely confident that they were going to do so. Instead they put in one of the most abject performances I think I've ever seen. I will never forgive them for that. But I'll never get to the point where I will not forgive the ace of diamonds for not hitting at a certain moment in blackjack. If I saw Russell Wilson tomorrow, I wouldn't bring it up with him. I'd be very amicable. I know it's completely irrational but I'd still want to blame him. It's the sort of drama around sport that you love and you live for. And no one does that better than the NFL.'

Although very few people successfully make a living from placing bets on sport, Ollie feels that the love of the NFL that betting ignited in him has made him a more thoughtful and skilled gambler. 'I learned very quickly when I first started gambling on soccer that I will always back my knowledge against that of most other people,' says Ollie. 'I work in sports broadcasting so I'm surrounded by people who specialise in particular sports. I'm never going to claim to know more about American football than Mike Carlson for example, that's basically impossible for me at this point. But at the same time, I would back myself against the bookie.

'What I've realised is that sport is inherently unpredictable. You have no idea if the quarterback might have had a bad night's sleep, which means that they're not going to perform well. So the way that I approach betting on the NFL now is about trying to spot value. That's where the handicap system becomes brilliant, because that lends itself to value and being able to identify it. With betting on the total, you can see how the bookmakers are rating each team against each other. It's all the scenarios in one number. You then decide whether that number is correct or not and place your bet accordingly. I love that because that is such a direct way to see it: "I think you put the wrong number so if I get this right, I'm beating you."'

The concept of value is part of the reason that the NFL has become so popular with British gamblers and why those gamblers have become dedicated fans of the sport. Ollie says an important aspect of this is that you can always have an evens bet on every game. This means that you can bet £1 and if you are right you win £1 and also get your £1 stake back. If a team in an NFL game is heavily favoured that may mean they are 13.5-point favourites. If you place £1 on them to cover that spread you need them to win by at least 14 points. Putting £1 on the other team means that as long as they lose by 13 points or fewer you have won £1 even if they don't win. 'That means you always get decent value,' says Ollie, 'provided you have looked into it and feel that the oddsmakers have given one team too much of an advantage. However, take soccer for instance, and a match between, say, Manchester City at home against Crystal Palace. Even if the odds are 100-1 there's absolutely no value there because it's so unlikely that Manchester City would lose. I don't think goals in soccer necessarily reflect the dominance of a team in the same way that I think points do in the NFL. Betting on the goalscorer market in soccer also puts you at a disadvantage compared with something similar in the NFL. You might find Mohamed Salah sometimes at evens to score two goals in a particular match. Whereas someone like Tyler Lockett to score two touchdowns for the Seattle Seahawks is sometimes 5-1 or 6-1. And yes, it's only going to happen maybe one in six or one in five games but the same applies to scoring two goals in a game but the odds are incredibly short for soccer. In the NFL the odds on offer better reflect what is likely to happen, at least in comparison with soccer. So that gives you the opportunity to win a lot more money and get a little bit more value.'

For a specific example, Ollie looks back at Super Bowl LVI, where he was in attendance to see his beloved Bengals lose to the Los Angeles Rams. 'Tee Higgins and Odell Beckham Jr both scored touchdowns in that game,' says Ollie. 'They were both the second-best wide receivers on teams that were known for their passing offenses. So you might have looked at them at the time in the same way you would look at Sadio Mané, with Salah at Liverpool at the time, and Manchester City's Kevin De Bruyne. The odds of both of them scoring would probably be like 3-1 or 4-1. However, Odell Beckham Jr was 8-1 so I bet on that immediately and won. All I saw in that was great value.

'Even if you've got a terrible game to watch and the points spread is big that doesn't mean the underdog won't cover. Look at the Jaguars when they played the Colts in the final regular season game of 2021. They were something like 14.5-point underdogs. It still looks like a decent bet. That means you can give yourself a reason to be enticed by the Jags, watch a struggling team and get invested in them, despite the fact that they've got nothing to play for at that point of the year and were a really bad team.'

From Ollie's perspective, Americans have made betting on the NFL socially acceptable very quickly. And although sports betting is incredibly common in the UK, it's often looked down upon. 'It's been glorified in the US compared with the UK and maybe that's because people want to celebrate it now it's legal. In the UK the culture surrounding sports gambling means that whenever people find out that it's one of my interests they say something like: "God, how much have you lost? That's such a bad habit." People often immediately assume you are addicted. Not enough people in the UK believe you can have a healthy relationship with it like you can with alcohol. People don't assume you're an alcoholic because they see you drinking a beer. The response in my head for these people is something along the lines of: "Yeah, OK, and how much have you spent on your stamp collection of whatever?" I have wasted much more money on drinking alcohol than I have gambling, I can tell you that.'

The Bears' star quarterback Jim McMahon sits on the sideline of the first American Bowl at Wembley in 1986. UK fans eventually grew tired of seeing backups take the majority of the snaps in these annual games and began to lose interest.

The Scottish Claymores and London Monarchs helped bring in more fans but many were left bitter when the teams eventually closed.

Things changed for UK fans forever in 2007 when the NFL finally started playing regular season games in London.

Every year fans across the UK attend special events to watch the biggest games together.

Fans would regularly flock to Regent Street in London when it would be closed off to host NFL celebrations.

Tottenham Hotspur Stadium has had mixed reviews from the UK's NFL fans. They love the facilities but its small size in comparison with Wembley means that many more people miss out on tickets.

Fans in the UK can now easily access a wide range of merchandise for all teams – unlike the limited selection on offer in the 1980s.

Almost 40 years to the week since Channel 4 launched, Wembley hosted an NFL game for the first time since 2019.

The new generation
bringing everyone together

NAVY BLUE. That's how it started for Liz Bhandari – better known to the British fan community as NFL Girl UK – in the very early days of her relationship with the man she would later marry. 'I remember going over to his place and he was watching a game,' says Liz. 'I can't remember what the game was but the Seattle Seahawks were on the screen. And that's where it started. I'm a big fan of the colour navy blue. I thought: Right, that's it, I'm making them my team.'

There was one potential obstacle: her new boyfriend was a San Francisco 49ers fan. 'I had no idea they were big divisional rivals,' admits Liz. 'He didn't try to convince me to support his team so that was good. But what I hate is that it's such a stereotypical girly thing to do, to choose a team because of its colours.'

Female fans have always had barriers put in front of them. Everything from having to justify why they're a fan or prove their knowledge of the game: things that male fans are never asked to do. What's more, is there really anything wrong with picking a team because you like how they look? After all, you're going to be watching them a lot and probably wearing their colours. There are countless male fans in the UK who will have picked a team based on this reason, in part because very few British people will have a geographic attachment to an NFL franchise. Liz has spent the past decade or so having to justify to some male fans why she should get to be involved in the community, and thankfully for everyone, it's not deterred her. One way or another it seems there have been forces trying to push her away from the sport she now loves.

'The first time I ever really paid attention to the NFL was when I stayed up to watch Beyoncé in the Super Bowl XLVII half-time show,' says Liz. 'I've since gone back and found what I said on Twitter at the time. It was something along the lines of American football just being rugby league with pads on. Obviously, a couple of years later I became an NFL fan but back then I really associated it with rugby league. I'm from a rugby league town and the NFL wasn't taken seriously there. Now I have to tell people: "Yes they've got pads on but they're also hitting people a lot harder."'

The days of Liz having misconceptions about what American football is or should be are long gone. But some UK fans still have their own idea about what she should be doing. 'Although I'm a Seahawks fan I still like other teams and players,' she says. 'I love the sport but I'm perhaps not the most die-hard Seahawks fan. So I will wear jerseys or whatever from other teams or players because I like them. And whenever I do there are people ready to rip the piss out of me on social media. Most of my followers on Twitter are men and they are fantastic. I'd say there is always a small handful of crazies around who just can't handle a girl talking about sport.'

Liz knows branding and her personal brand has become something other than being a high-profile Seahawks fan so it's entirely forgivable if her focus strays to the other 31 teams as well. 'I've always loved to write,' says Liz, 'and that's where this all started. I wanted to write about the NFL in general and what it was like being a fan. I didn't have my NFL Girl UK Twitter account at this point, so I was just doing it from my personal account. The majority of my followers were just people I knew from Warrington, so I decided to create a whole new account. I thought: "I'm going to cover the NFL, I'm a girl and I'm in the UK." That's as much thought as went into the name. I started off with a free WordPress website just before the Detroit Lions and Atlanta Falcons played at Wembley in 2014. That was the first game I ever went to.'

The website grew and Liz decided that the site could be more than just her own thoughts. 'I paid for my own hosting and bought the domain name,' she says. 'Then I thought it would be quite nice to learn from other fans about how they got into the game. I got fans of different teams to take over and share their stories. From there, I started to get other people who were keen to start writing. I was happy for them to write about anything as long as it was to do with the NFL. I was always very conscious of the fact that because it was all coming out of my website and my social media account I was the one getting credit for it all.'

The result was Liz launching Ninety-Nine Yards, an outlet for aspiring American football writers to tackle their favourite sport. 'I've loved giving people that platform,' says Liz. 'And we've seen people go on to bigger and better things, which is exciting.' The other benefit was that Liz could use her original site just for her own projects and ideas. This included creating her first podcast off the back of interviews she was doing. 'The interviews were always recorded,' she says, 'and they were part of a "Day in the life of ..." series. Podcasting was becoming more of a thing so it just felt like the right time. I made the decision to turn it into a podcast series and I've really enjoyed doing that.'

Liz's Cleats Off podcast has featured plenty of big names from the NFL world, such as *NFL RedZone* host Scott Hanson ('that bundle of energy is real'), but it's also been a place to spotlight some of the women who have an impact on the sport. These have included Connie Carberg, the first female scout in NFL history; Laura Okmin, the NFL sideline reporter who runs the GALvanize sports media training programme for women; Lori Locust, the Super Bowl-winning assistant defensive line coach hired by Bruce Arians at the Tampa Bay Buccaneers; and Erica Tamposi, producer of the hit podcast Around The NFL.

'Many of these women have "first" titles, but in reality the numbers of women in the game are still small,' Liz says. 'It's only recently we've seen any female coaches on the sideline or officiating. The women I've spoken to can't wait for this whole "first female to …" description to no longer be a thing. I use the description myself to say I'm one of the first female NFL podcasters and bloggers in the UK because that's what helps me stand out. Nowadays anyone can make a podcast if they really want to, so being able to say something like that is quite special.

'The NFL – and sports as a whole – obviously still has such a long way to go with it. I think the reason is because many people still have an old-school mentality and are of the opinion that you shouldn't be in a coaching session unless you've played the sport. But many NFL coaches haven't really played. It's taken programmes to be put in place for there to be any progressive change. It's not just a lack of women in positions of power across the NFL, it's people of colour as well. There's a lack of certain people because of a lack of opportunity. The NFL is taking the right steps in terms of getting more women into the league, but like with anything, it takes time for people to buy into it. On the other hand you have people such as Bruce Arians who hired Jen Welter as the first female coach ever in the NFL when he was at the Arizona Cardinals, then later when he joined the Tampa Bay Buccaneers he opened up the opportunity again to hire more women.'

As much as Liz has done to celebrate female empowerment in the sport, many fans in the UK associate her with her meetups more than her work bringing women into the game. Whether it's the famous Christmas parties or the events scheduled around International Series games in London, many fans will plan their diaries around Liz's big nights. 'The first was in Manchester and I just wanted to see if people actually wanted to do this,' says Liz. 'The plan was mini golf and fried chicken, and ten people turned up. It was a really small group but I thought it was a good start. I'd gotten into events because part of my day job at the time was marketing events for an accountant.

'The next one was in 2017, the night before an NFL game in London. This time there were 40 people, which was amazing. It was a really nice environment – I met some people I'd been speaking to on Twitter for years and also people I didn't even know. I soon started thinking about the following year. I built a relationship with the team at All Star Lanes in Brick Lane in London and I hired its private room for three consecutive Saturday nights in 2018 ahead of games in London.

'The first weekend ahead of the Seahawks playing the Raiders we had about 60 people. My thought at the time was that I had hired a venue that was too big. Then the second week came along, with the Tennessee Titans playing the Los Angeles Chargers. A massive group from Germany came over and I think they bought about 60 tickets. In total we had 130 people, which is the maximum capacity. It was a crazy atmosphere. I don't think I've ever seen an event like that, that I've ever hosted myself. And I'm not sure I ever will see an event like that again. For the final week, for the Philadelphia Eagles and Jacksonville Jaguars, it was about 80 people. I was exhausted after that. I realised it was too much. I don't live in London so I would have to come down on Friday, so I could fit everything in.

'The next year, I simplified it. We went to Flight Club for darts and then went somewhere else for drinks afterwards. You can only get about 50 or 60 people in at Flight Club so that limited our numbers. I didn't want to go crazy again. For the 2021 games after the pandemic I went to Sports Bar & Grill in Marylebone and we pretty much had their basement area to ourselves. I wanted people to use it as an opportunity for small fan groups to come along and gather in their own corners. We've started to get Americans coming along as well.'

The meetups have been well appreciated by fans, eager to talk NFL over drinks with new friends – something that is unlikely to happen in their day-to-day lives. Liz is hoping to do even more for them. 'I'd love to see the meetups become more like the NFL UK Live events,' says Liz, referencing the special evenings the league's London office has taken around the country to host interactive Q&As with players and coaches. 'Whether I can actually make that happen is a different story. But I'd love to have a special guest who we can interview. I've done that a bit with the annual Christmas meetups, thanks to [coach and frequent Sky Sports guest] Jeff Reinebold. He has pretty much been to every single one of the events and always ends up answering questions from the fans.'

As well as being a moderator for the main NFL UK Facebook group, Liz is also involved in a group just for female fans. 'There would be certain points in the main group where female fans I spoke to were worried that if they said the wrong thing in some way then the crazies would criticise them,' says Liz. 'So I built my own group and we have 400 people. The majority are from the UK, but there are definitely a few Americans as well. I wanted somewhere

where we could say whatever the hell we wanted, and not have someone call us out for a stupid reason. It's a shame that's what was needed because it's certainly not all the fans in the main group causing a problem, it's just the occasional one or two that can disrupt it for everyone else. There are other female-led groups around and I love all of that kind of stuff. It's nice to have a space that women feel they can use without feeling judged or falling into the trap of imposter syndrome where you don't feel like you can talk about a subject. You think you're not as knowledgeable so you let other people speak for you. And it's very easy to fall into that because I've done that myself a million times.

'In 2021 NFL UK's Her Huddle launched on YouTube and Instagram Live, and is now a Sky Sports TV show and podcast. It's hosted by [Sky Sports presenter] Hannah Wilkes, but both myself and Ash Byrne-Hansen [from podcast Ash and the NFL] are guest hosts on that. Realistically it's a show by women for women, but at no point do we ever say men can't watch it! We're all about having allies and people who will help champion women in sport. So I think that's really important. The stats in America show that nearly 50 per cent of NFL fans are female. I think the difference is it's unusual to have women leading the conversation over here. I'm still seeing a lot more men talk about American football than I see women, which is a shame, but it will grow. It takes having people like Hannah Wilkes in the spotlight or [Olympic hockey gold medallist] Sam Quek hosting at London games. Sometimes women are put in particular roles where they don't get the chance to showcase their knowledge. Then the assumption is that they're just on TV because they're pretty or something like that.'

While almost half of NFL fans in America are women, the UK lags behind. A YouGov survey in 2022 found that

THE AMERICAN FOOTBALL REVOLUTION

73 per cent of the UK's NFL fans are male. This is a bigger disparity than seen by the NBA, where 67 per cent of UK fans are male, and MLB, where the number is 68 per cent. A separate YouGov survey from 2020 found that 75 per cent of all sports fans in the UK are male. Although there is an imbalance with the NFL Liz feels things are moving in the right direction. 'It's not just American football, it's a majority of sports,' she says. 'Look at how many people moan about soccer in the UK when there's a female presenter. The amount of crap a woman on TV gets for voicing one opinion that's different to the one someone watching has is ridiculous. Same for female soccer referees. Clearly these women know the sport otherwise they wouldn't put themselves through it.

'When it comes to American football we're fairly lucky because it's quite ordinary for a woman to be a sideline reporter and there are women working on major NFL TV shows. Here in the UK, when Dara Kennedy took over as the main NFL host on Sky Sports from Kevin Cadle, she got so much hate. I must admit she did make quite a few mistakes and as a fan that was frustrating. Now, [current host] Neil Reynolds gets criticism as well – just look at how people blame him because they don't like the schedule as if he's personally responsible – but the women are always going to be the ones who get called out first. I think there are some NFL UK fans who you can never make happy. It doesn't matter.'

For the sport's high-profile female fans in the UK there is a level of pressure for them to represent their gender within the community. If they do something that makes them look bad there's a fear that will reflect on all women who love the game. 'I've certainly felt the pressure,' says Liz. 'It's quite difficult sometimes on Sundays to focus on the games, because I'm so preoccupied with what's happening on social media. A few years ago I admitted on social media that I didn't stay up late to watch a Seahawks game. I got absolutely slaughtered by a couple of guys. "Are you not a true fan?" All that kind of stuff. Guys, I need my sleep. Obviously I stay up for the Super Bowl. Thanksgiving is no problem either. But for the rest of the year, I am going to bed at 11pm because I need my sleep.'

The worry that she wasn't being a good enough fan has weighed heavy on Liz at times despite everything she has done. One particular scary moment was when she was pitted against other fans in a public space and put her knowledge up against theirs. 'In 2021 outside one of the games at Tottenham I was filmed doing a quiz with three guys,' says Liz. 'We were all filmed individually and I was really feeling nervous about it. I worried that I wouldn't know as much as other people because I've not been a fan as long as some have. For the quiz they would do things like bring up a person on screen and you couldn't fully see their face. I had to pass on quite a few people. Afterwards the people filming said to me: "Oh, that was great. That's brilliant." But I walked away and cried because I had to pass on so many.

'I bawled my eyes out because I was so scared that people were going to see me for a fraud. I've been building this audience for years and what do I actually know about this sport? Like my whole thing was just some kind of act. When they gave the results I came second. I thought I would be last but there was only one point between me and the guy who actually won it. It's just funny how that kind of stuff kicks in. It's a confidence thing. I admit to anyone on Twitter that I don't know everything, and I don't pretend to know everything either. It's just that there is pressure in my head sometimes.

'I have turned down radio interviews, because I think I've simply been scared that they would ask me something and I wouldn't know the answer. I'm sure I'm not the only one who feels like that. One time I was on The Nat Coombs Show podcast and some guy was criticising me on Twitter after it. And Nat defended me immediately, which meant a lot. One of the things I love about Nat is that not only is he open to giving people opportunities, he'll stand up for what's right.'

Liz has been very effective in maximising those opportunities when they come her way and it even encouraged her to start her own side-hustle business, Brandari, in 2020. Within two years she had quit her day job to focus on Brandari full-time. 'During 2021 I reached out to brands to see if they would like me to write NFL content for them. I've worked with retailers, bars, restaurants and betting companies for example. I'm not a betting expert in the slightest, but I can confidently write and talk about a game. In the past that wasn't really an avenue I considered going down but now working with brands is absolutely something I want to do.

'If I can make an income talking about American football, then that's kind of a dream, right? There was this time Papa John's did a campaign around the NFL and I shared the hell out of it on social media and then I gave them ideas of what other things the brand should be doing. Papa John's ended up giving me free tickets for one of the Wembley games – and it was Club Wembley, so that's not the hospitality boxes but it's the comfy seats and the cup holders. That kind of gave me a taste of what was possible.

'At that time I already had years of experience in marketing. I've always wanted to get involved in marketing around American football or doing something connected from a brand perspective. I've built my audience on social media and the podcast and whatnot. This has opened doors for me so I have brands reaching out to me every now and again, which is amazing. If there's a career that could be built from it through my own business that's 100 per cent the way I want to do it. That's why I left my full-time job in order to do all of this. Working for myself gives me more headspace and time to do things like player interviews or going to media days. That gives me a chance to really step up my game because I won't have the day job distracting me. It's nice when I can spend a morning creating content for NFL stuff if I want to rather than juggling it around other responsibilities.'

As well as the marketing side, Liz hopes the added freedom will allow her to expand the NFL Girl UK website and help bring in another generation of female American football fans. 'I would love for it to become the main destination for female fans who want to learn about the sport, whether it's the basics of the game or understand more of the terminology,' says Liz. 'That would be awesome because there isn't really anything out there like that. From a writing point of view, I would love to have a full team of writers so we have one female fan per team writing content about the sport.

'I'd love to do more with the podcast as well. It's hard to get noticed by some teams because I'm just not big enough for them. They won't give me the time of day. And that's fine, I'm just one small outlet in the UK. But I would love to be in a position where I am interviewing a player from a different team each week. I want to open up the platform, like I did with Ninety-Nine Yards, but for women. NFL Girl UK as a website can go one of two ways. It can be just about me or I can make it all women. It needs to be one of those two routes.'

Although almost everyone would acknowledge the need to help new fans get into the sport and learn the rules, there has also been a battle within the UK in which many dedicated fans get angry about the way that major news providers such as Sky Sports, BBC Sport or the NFL's UK office 'dumb things down' for new or prospective fans. Liz feels this criticism is unwarranted and unhelpful. 'Their content isn't really for the advanced fan,' she says, 'it's aimed at getting new people into the sport as much as possible because that is what's going to sustain the NFL especially if one day we do have our own franchise. A lot of these newer fans are the ones who will be buying season tickets if that ever happens. I understand NFL UK's position and why they have to market themselves in that way. I don't always necessarily agree with how they do it but from a marketing point of view, yeah, that's absolutely how it has to be done.'

Each year when tickets for the International Series games in London go on sale they are the hottest tickets around. Many fans are left disappointed despite the games being held in big stadiums.

For fans who miss out on seeing their favourite team it's a bitter pill to swallow. This is magnified when they see celebrities and British stars of other sports – who have previously shown no interest in the NFL – paraded around as guests of honour and given free tickets. It's not an issue unique to the NFL. The NBA suffered the same criticism when it used to play regular season games in London. Meanwhile, when Major League Baseball debuted its Home Run Derby X exhibition format in London, it had people such as massively popular FIFA-esports-star-turned-soccer-influencer Spencer Owen actually taking part on the field for the Chicago Cubs, with freestyle soccer player and TikTok superstar Liv Cooke playing for the Los Angeles Dodgers, much to the chagrin of existing baseball fans in the UK. At the very least the NFL can be given credit for trusting fans in the UK to sit through a real American football game, something MLB is still not confident about happening on a regular basis for baseball.

Don't expect to see anything like this from Liz, however. She wants to build her business and her personal brand with a view to encouraging as many new fans as possible, especially women, to give the sport a chance. She may have become a very visible fan in the community thanks to her websites, social media presence and platform on Her Huddle but it's never about shining a light on herself. 'I've got no intention of being an Instagram influencer or anything like that, it was never my intention,' says Liz. 'I don't want to be famous or anything like that. I just enjoy writing and sharing people's stories.'

UK fans invade the US

ATTENDING AN NFL game isn't exactly easy – even if you live in the US. It's expensive and tickets aren't always readily available. If you don't live near the stadium you have to factor in how you're going to get there. If it's going to be a long journey back you may need to find a hotel. If you're travelling from the UK it's going to be an expensive round trip even if you find cheap tickets and end up sleeping on an American friend's sofa. Despite this, many fans make the pilgrimage each year. Firms such as Touchdown Trips have sprung up to take groups to multiple games in a single trip during which they can meet other like-minded obsessives from the UK.

Some people, such as Jacob Barnor, spent years dreaming of seeing an NFL game stateside before they got to do it. 'My first memory of American football is playing *Madden NFL 06* with my mate,' says Jacob. 'It was his game and I didn't really know what the hell was going on when I played it. Years later I decided I should watch Super Bowl XLVI between the Giants and Patriots. However, I watched highlights the next day because I was a kid and I wasn't going to stay up all night to watch it live.'

Jacob liked what he saw and wanted to see more games, checking out the Sunday evening matches on Sky Sports. At the very least, he says, 'I would then have half an idea of what I was doing on *Madden*.'

If he was going to watch, then he wanted to have a team. 'I started watching more and more. I fell in love with it. I became a 49ers fan because of my dad,' says Jacob. 'When I was younger, he sometimes had to work abroad. He worked for [tech company] Oracle and one of their offices was in San Francisco so he used to go over there every now and again. He'd normally bring me back some San Francisco-themed gifts so I already had some 49ers stuff. So I decided I would make a point of watching 49ers games. The first one I saw, they won. I liked their quarterback Alex Smith so that was enough for me. They actually had a really bad season but at least I saw one of the wins. When you're a foreign fan, you've not got that tie of being born there. You have to look for any sort of tie you've got. That makes you as much of a fan as anybody else.'

When Jacob throws himself into something, he really throws himself into it. He had plans to attend the University of Birmingham and join its successful American football team, the Lions. Jacob didn't want to turn up unprepared so he joined a local team to get himself ready. 'The very first team I played for was Leeds Bobcats under-19s,' he says. 'I had already done MMA for a few years but had decided to look for a team sport. I knew I wanted to go to Birmingham and I also knew they had one of the best teams in the country. I didn't want to turn up having no idea what it's like to play so I joined a local junior team. At least that way I wouldn't be completely clueless. However, I ended up getting injured while with the Bobcats and having surgery on my hip. I missed out on playing in Birmingham during my first season there because of it. I was there for every practice though, watching everything like I was in a classroom.

'Because I couldn't physically play, I was trying to put as much as I could into the mental side of the game so that when I came back I could hit the ground running. I spent so much time studying the game and watching film.

I think that's what took it to that next level for me, because suddenly, I was trying to understand all the intricacies of the sport. In Birmingham we were lucky to have some of the best coaches in the country. We had a positional coach for every position.'

Jacob's time as a Lion was important away from his team's games too. He was surrounded by NFL fans. 'Our "Sunday Funday" was a huge, huge part of the culture there,' says Jacob. 'After my first year, I lived with people from the team so I always had that group. There was a bar that used to sponsor the team and they would essentially open on Sunday evening just for the players to watch the NFL on the big screen. We usually had games on a Saturday and we'd follow that with a night out. Then Sunday would be spent hungover and watching the NFL.'

While time spent watching film or NFL games on TV gave Jacob a greater appreciation for American football, it was a chance trip to an International Series game not long after starting university that inadvertently kick-started an adventure. 'One of my friends from school got two tickets to the 49ers vs Jaguars game at Wembley in 2013 for his birthday,' says Jacob. 'I was the person he knew who was most into the sport so he invited me to come along. That was my first ever live game. When the teams come to the UK they usually run Play 60 sessions for local kids. In the years after my first International Series game, my university was often asked to help out at those sessions. We would come down to London to look after the kids and sometimes get to watch a bit of practice. Some of the players would stick around to help you. It might be star players or practice squad players, but it was such a cool opportunity either way. As a thank you for helping, we'd often be given tickets to the London games as well.

'I'd only ever really been to soccer matches at the time and the NFL experience was totally different. The first thing that struck me and I know a lot of people say this, is that you'll see every single jersey at a London game. I thought that was really cool to see. It feels like in the early years of the International Series, we had more people who were just intrigued and didn't have as much of an idea of what was going on. And I'm including myself at the time compared to where I am now. The sport has grown so much that pretty much everyone at the games nowadays is properly into the NFL. People aren't there because it's a novelty.'

After four years Jacob came home to Leeds with his degree and he wanted to stay involved in the sport he now loved. 'I got a job with Sky Bet and played an adult season with the Yorkshire Rams after graduation,' he says. 'Then I had to hang it up thanks to too many injuries but I was also the linebackers coach for Leeds Beckett University. One thing I realised very quickly is the incredible time commitment coaches put in. As a player, you think you're making a big time commitment but most players don't really appreciate that the coaches are probably putting in even more time while working full-time as well. It was important to me to do something for students like coaches had done for me in Birmingham.'

Jacob's job saw him focusing a lot on the NFL side of the betting service so he was very busy during the American football season. This was a problem for someone who harboured ambitions of seeing a pro game stateside. 'In my final year of university, I went to America and got to a college game: UCLA vs Stanford at the Rose Bowl,' says Jacob, 'but I didn't see an NFL game. At that point I was determined to see one over there in the future. Being able to get time off during the NFL season wasn't the easiest when I was working at Sky Bet, though. One of my best mates is a Denver Broncos fan and in 2018 we were thinking about the fact that the Broncos were playing the 49ers that year. We had a conversation about whether we should just see if we can get time off and go. I begged work to let me have a week off during the season and they did. So off we went. We did the Niners game, we did a Golden State Warriors basketball game and we did a San Jose Sharks ice hockey game.'

It clearly wasn't enough for Jacob to just go to a single game. His week became a tour of California's Bay Area taking in Santa Clara's Levi's Stadium, Oakland's Oracle Arena (another connection to his father) and San Jose's SAP Center. It was a sign of things to come. 'I remember coming back from that trip thinking: "I need to do more of this because this is next level." I thought the International Series at Wembley was different to anything I'd ever seen. This was well beyond that. I started to think I'd like to go to every NFL stadium and wondered how many I could do each year to gradually tick them off over the course of my life. I thought that maybe I would do an annual trip and visit two, three or four stadiums each time.

'At Sky Bet we worked a bit with *Gridiron* magazine and the staff were telling me all about their trips to the Super Bowl. I remember thinking I needed a job that meant I was the one going to the games rather than stuck in the office working. At that point I looked up people who had done all the stadiums because I knew I wasn't going to be the first person to have done that. I loved reading other people's stories about their trips. When I was Googling it, an article came up about a woman from Ohio who had managed to visit every stadium in the space of 86 days. It was like a light switch went on in my brain. I knew that's what I had to do.'

Getting to every NFL stadium over the course of a season sounds like a dream for any fan. Doing it in record time might sound more like a pipe dream. As much as Jacob loved the idea of attempting it there were many obstacles to overcome. 'I'm definitely known for having big ideas that I probably never execute on,' admits Jacob. 'I would often tell myself I was going to do something but never actually finish it. From the beginning this felt a little bit different. I had broken up with my girlfriend about six or seven months prior, and was not in the greatest headspace at the time. I wanted to do something just for me that made me happy because I wasn't at the time.

'That prompted me to look into whether it was really possible to accomplish. What do I need to do? How much money would I need? All that sort of stuff. Eventually I started planting the seed with my friends to see what people thought. A lot of people thought I was batshit crazy. Just another of my big ideas that would never come to anything. When I mentioned it to my parents, however, they were totally supportive because they were both big travellers. They told me it sounded incredible and that I should definitely do it. I needed to hear that.'

Emotional support helped legitimise the idea in Jacob's head but it wasn't all he needed. The trip would be expensive and would require him to miss the vast majority of the NFL regular season in a job where that was the busiest time. If getting just one week off was tricky, how would he pull off a three-month break? 'I knew that if I went into work and said: "Can I have three months off during the NFL season?" the answer would be no. That was not the smart approach,' says Jacob. 'So I told my manager: "I'm going to do this. If my job is here for me when I come back, that's great. That'd be the ideal situation. However, if it's not, I completely understand."

Their attitude was: "Well, if you're going to do it anyway, we might as well have you back afterwards." That was very, very, very good for me!

'There were some people who couldn't believe I had pulled it off because it was definitely unheard of. There were schemes at the company whereby if you'd been there a certain amount of time, you were eligible to have like a year's sabbatical for travelling or whatever but I hadn't worked there long enough. A lot of companies would have said my job was gone so huge props to my employer for doing this. It took the pressure off in a big way. I took some of the three months as holiday but most of it was unpaid leave.'

So the trip was on. It was doable. Expensive but doable. He had been saving for a house deposit but now that money would be used for the trip. Luckily some useful advice was just a phone call away. 'I spoke to Adam Goldstein because of his tailgating trip,' says Jacob. 'I said to him: "I'd love any help! Whether that's ins you've got with tailgates or just any advice." We had a two-hour conversation about his experience, tips for dealing with it all and things he would have done differently if he went again. He was hugely helpful.'

The NFL UK community had come through for him. But as much effort as Jacob was putting in to make this work, it was only going to be possible if the schedule allowed him to tick off all the stadiums in time. Ahead of the NFL's schedule release day there are always leaks to whet the appetite of fans. But very few people were going to be studying the whole thing like Jacob was. 'That was a big night for me,' he says. 'Because at the end of the day, if the schedule is not right, I can't break the world record. However, at that point, I was committed. I was going to make the trip anyway. If it's not for the record, I'm still going to go to every stadium in three months, or however long it takes. That would still be a cool story. I wanted to chase the record because doing it gave the trip a bigger purpose. I figured it would probably help me in the sort of things I needed to do. I knew if I was ever stuck for tickets, the fact I was aiming for a world record was an easy story to use.'

The schedule was revealed at 1am UK time and Jacob started plotting it all out. 'At that point I knew where I had to be every Thursday and Monday night, that didn't matter or change,' he says. 'The problem was the Sunday games because I had to find the easiest route. Ideally, you want a Sunday game that is taking place somewhere in between those Thursday and Monday night games. So for the first game of the season I knew I was in Chicago. Monday, I'm in New Orleans. Where can I go on that Sunday to make the trip easier? The simplest option was Dallas. It was a matter of going through that process for each. Sometimes I'd go through it all, reach something like week 10 and realise it would leave me with a really difficult end of the trip. So it's back to the drawing board.

'Towards the end, I ended up having to squeeze some in. I did something like Sunday was Cincinnati, Monday was LA and Thursday was Atlanta. That's not a good way to do it but that sort of hassle had to happen at some point. What determines how quickly you can do it boils down to how often they repeat the Thursday and then Monday venues. So for example, when I was doing it, there were two Jets home games on *Monday Night Football* in the first seven weeks, which meant that was a whole gameday where I couldn't go to a new stadium, even though it could potentially help me break the record quicker. I was adamant that I didn't want to do two games in a single day. I knew how hard it can be to get in and out of stadiums. I wanted the record but I also wanted to have the best time possible. I knew I would be so stressed about getting from an early game on a Sunday to the night game later that day. It just wasn't worth it because I wasn't planning on leaving any games early.'

Another thing Jacob decided to avoid in favour of just enjoying himself was vlogging. This was a fun trip not a work trip, even though he knew proper videos could be very popular – and potentially lucrative. 'I didn't want to be somewhere worrying about the shot,' says Jacob, 'or worrying about what's in front of the camera or watching things though a phone screen. It would have made for unbelievable content, there's no doubt about that. In that sense, I wish I had maybe created more content around it. Although it's not much fun if you're trying to take a shot, but also worry that you sound really drunk. I didn't want to worry about that. The ideal situation would have been having someone else there to film it with me, but financially that would never have been an option. I did look into sponsors and if someone had asked me ahead of time to make content in exchange for them covering half the cost or something like that then I would have certainly considered it.'

After figuring out which games he needed to attend, Jacob had to plot a route criss-crossing the US that would also allow him to fit in some sightseeing. 'For example,' says Jacob, 'when it came to the New York game that I went to on a Monday night, I just left straight away because I had been to New York before. However, when I was in New Orleans, I got there Monday morning, went to the game that night, but actually wanted to see the city properly. For that one I flew out on Wednesday morning because that way even if your morning flight is delayed or cancelled, you've got Wednesday afternoon or potentially fly out the next day to reach the Thursday game. It would be a lie to say I enjoyed every single day. There were weeks where I'd done a Saturday college game, been to a Sunday NFL game and the last thing I wanted to do was go to *Monday Night Football* the next night! The one thing that stayed with me though was that a lot of people would kill to be at just this one game. So I did appreciate it.'

Financially, things were proving tough and other things were taking their toll. Jacob did cost out the trip ahead of time but he soon realised he had been rather optimistic. 'I needed more flights than I realised,' admits Jacob. 'I was spending more money than I planned along the way. About two weeks into the trip, I remember thinking: "OK, I can't sustain this." There were times where I was just absolutely knackered. I would sometimes tell my friends back home how tired I was and they would say: "You're off having the best time ever – you can't be tired!" Then the same friends would come out to visit me for a week or so to join me for a bit of the trip and tell me they didn't know how I could cope with the non-stop travelling for 12 weeks. It was three flights a week and I was constantly on the move. I would never get a home-cooked meal. And eventually it caught up with me and I got so ill I thought I was going to miss a game. There was a point in Arizona where I wasn't sure if I could get through the game without throwing up. Thankfully I made it.'

Jacob became a travelling ambassador, showing Americans how dedicated UK NFL fans could be. 'I really shocked them,' he says. 'A lot of people didn't believe me until I showed them all my social media stuff. A lot of times Americans assume British people don't know that much about this sport. And I don't blame them because I probably do the same thing when I hear an American talk about soccer. Once the American fans realised I knew what I was talking about and that it was realistic for me to break the record they were so excited. Especially the people at the tailgates. It really helped me capture what I wanted to experience. I tried to avoid 49ers road games because I knew I would be a 49ers fan that day. That wouldn't help me get the unique home team experience.'

After weeks of travelling the record was finally in sight. The final game would be at Mercedes-Benz Stadium in Atlanta on Thanksgiving night. 'In the build-up to that game it felt like my story was really starting to blow up back home,' says Jacob. 'I had already appeared on lots of podcasts during the trip but it had fallen to me to organise those so I could spread the word. Eventually it flipped and people were approaching me instead. Maybe some people didn't believe a British fan could actually do it at the beginning. In the run-up to the final game I had some friends join me and I needed their help. Between us we had to schedule a day full of interviews. It was so bizarre. My friends would tell me: "OK, you've the BBC at this time. Then you're going to the CNN studio in Atlanta a little bit after this. You've got Sky Sports in the morning." I can't imagine I'll ever experience anything like all that again. I did three or four hours of interviews on the day of the game itself. The Falcons reached out to me beforehand saying they were really excited that I would be breaking the record in their stadium.'

The Falcons planned to push the boat out for Jacob and make the night as memorable as possible. 'They gave me pregame passes and said they had a surprise for me,' says Jacob. 'I was given a signed Matt Ryan jersey and I thought that was the surprise! When it came to signing the form to prove to Guinness World Records that I had been at the game it was someone high up in the Falcons organisation who wanted to do that bit of paperwork. As we were chatting he said quite casually: "By the way, you're going to the Super Bowl."'

On an already emotional and exhausting day Jacob was stunned. 'I could see an NFL Films camera crew,' he says, 'and I was then given a gold NFL football with a message saying I was going to the Super Bowl. I turned around and my two friends were holding giant novelty tickets like those big fake cheques people pose with when they win the lottery. I didn't know what to say. Then I started to get worried because I had no money left. I had no idea how I was going to pay for a flight to the Super Bowl or find a hotel that wasn't super expensive. It wasn't until the next day when a video of it was posted on Twitter that I realised that the NFL was covering all those costs for me!'

The offer of a trip to the Super Bowl was just what Jacob needed. Of course, any fan would love it but it came at just the right time for Jacob because finishing this epic record-breaking journey left him with one very important question: 'Now what?' At least he knew that in less than ten weeks he had an all-expenses-paid trip to the biggest game of the season to look forward to. By now he was running on empty. The cliche of 'it's not the destination, it's the journey' had never been so true. 'For three months, I had dedicated my life to this trip,' he says. 'It was the only thing that mattered and then it was done. It was a weird feeling. The Super Bowl trip really helped because it was almost like the journey wasn't actually over.'

The trip had cost Jacob around £20,000, although his Super Bowl trip was probably worth a similar amount ('It's like I bought a trip to see the 49ers in the Super Bowl and got an extra three-month trip out of it for free,' he jokes) and it was time to get back to work. Jacob had applied for a job in the US and interviewed for it during the trip. He was offered the position although Covid delayed him moving out to LA to start. 'Although there ended up being quite a wait, it meant that I felt my next adventure was already on the horizon,' says Jacob. 'I wasn't simply going back to my same job back home, sitting there thinking: "I had the best time ever and now I'm back to this." That would've been hard.

'In America the record comes up a lot when I meet someone. I'm not sick of it because if nothing else it's one of the best icebreakers in the world. When I meet people at tailgates now and it comes up, people are interested. Other fans want to know what type of person would try to do such a thing. It was the best time of my life, so however often I get to relive it is great. I try not to bring it up all the time but it's useful to know it's there.'

With Jacob now based in LA, he's been able to revisit cities that he only paid flying visits to during his record-breaking trip. 'I went to 49ers playoff games in January 2022 and I managed to go to Green Bay. The nice thing now about living here is I can go back to the places I really, really enjoyed but didn't get the time to really appreciate. I went to Chicago for a long weekend when the 49ers played there in week one of the 2022 season, which was great to do despite the monsoon and result.'

Jacob became a hero to the UK fan community with his adventure. Not content with simply inspiring others, he's become a font of knowledge for anyone who wants to travel from the UK to the US for an NFL tour. 'I've been asked everything,' says Jacob. 'I've had a lot of questions about tailgates. When I go to a lot of these tailgates, they love the fact that people are spreading the word and sending fans from all over the world to them. People also get in touch to say they want to break my record and ask me for some help, which I've been happy to provide.

'As much as I'd love to keep the record forever, I would never want to prevent somebody from having the opportunity and experience that I had. I tell them all if they're able to do it, just do it and you won't regret it. You'll have the best time of your life. The stories that you'll have are so unique that it makes up for the hard work. You would never get to experience these things outside the NFL.'

Acknowledgements

FIRSTLY THANKS to Jane Camillin, along with everyone else at Pitch Publishing who made this book happen. There was no other imprint I wanted to work with on this project. Other great Pitch books such as *American Football's Forgotten Kings: The Rise and Fall of the London Monarchs* by Nick Cassidy and *The Special Relationship: The History of American Football in the United Kingdom* by Andrew Gamble are both recommended if you enjoyed this book.

Thanks to all the pioneers who ensured there were great publications to read in the 1980s. The likes of *First Down*, *Gridiron*, *Touchdown* and *Quarterback* not only fed my interest in the sport but also made me want to work on magazines.

Thank you to the NFL itself for realising the potential outside the US and creating the UK office. Without that I'm not sure where we'd be.

Thanks to Mike Carlson who crafted the most perfect foreword I could have dreamed of. No person came up more in interviews for this book than Mike and he was the only person I wanted for the foreword. Mike, thank you for saying yes and for being such an icon for UK fans. His Patreon newsletter, Friday Morning Tight End, is essential reading for all NFL fans and I encourage you all to check it out at patreon.com/mikecarlsonfmte

A shoutout to all the people I talk to on social media about American football on a daily basis. I'd love to list you all by name but the book would end up double the size if I did. You are all doing a valuable job making the sport what it is over here.

A word of appreciation for everyone who ever booked me for a podcast, radio or TV appearance. It was a bit surreal talking live on BBC TV from my living room the morning after a Super Bowl while my wife and daughter kept the dogs out of barking range. Thanks to Will Gavin for ensuring I never go too long between appearances on talkSPORT2. You don't need me to tell you the impact your commitment to the sport has had on the UK because of everything you work on: the radio station, the modern *Gridiron* magazine and more.

Thank you to everyone who gave up their time to be interviewed for this book. All your stories were fascinating, as evidenced by how long we spent talking each time. I also appreciate you spreading the word about the book and helping it reach as wide an audience as possible.

Credit must also go to every person, outlet, podcast and website that have helped promote the book, including but not limited to, the Waxing Lyrical podcast (@Waxing_Lyrical), Andy Devaney at Sustain Health magazine (sustainhealth. fit), Cameron Hobbs and Paul W Mitchell from the Stramash! podcast (nflscotland.com), Liam O'Neill, Mik McGivern and Phill Mountstephens from the British and Irish Eagles (british-eagles.com), Iain, Jake and Dave from the WINFL Show (@TheWINFLShow), Tom Kingham at ESPN (ESPN.co.uk), Seb Kennedy from Seb Talks Sports (@SebTalksSports), the entire Full 10 Yards Network (full10yards.co.uk), Nathan Dowie and the team at the Fields of Fantasy: NFL podcast (@FoFNFLUK), Roar of the Lions UK (roarofthelionsuk.com), Duncan Terry and the team at Ninety-Nine Yards (ninetynineyards.com), Touchdown Tips (touchdowntips.com), Freddie Hall, Adam Martin, Andrew

Manning and Gareth Smith from The Franchise Tag Podcast (thefranchisetag.co.uk), Jack Brentnall at The Jet Sweep (the-jet-sweep.com), Tony Wheat at Full Press Commanders (@FPC_Commanders) and collectibles website Stateside Sports (statesidesports.co.uk). All of them are supporting and uplifting the NFL UK community and deserve your support in return.

Finally, thank you to everyone who has supported the sport, no matter what country you live in or are from. It's a special game and it changed my life.